BEWARE THE NEW PROPHETS

A Caution Concerning

The Prophetic Movement

by

Pastor Bill Randles

"And what will you do in the end?"

First published in the USA in 1999

Copyright © Bill Randles 1999
ISBN 0 9646626 3 9

Further copies of this booklet are available in some bookstores or can be ordered from:
Pastor Bill Randles
8600 C Ave
Marion
IOWA 52302
Tel: 319 373 3898

CONTENTS

Introduction

By Jacob Prasch

When the Lord Jesus, the Apostles, and the Hebrew prophets repeatedly warned of the emergence of false prophets in the last days, most Christians have taken that to mean to non-Christian and pseudo-Christian cults outside of the Body of Christ. To most of us it means the Mormons, The Jehovah's Witnesses, the Unification Church, Christian Scientists or some other clearly heretical group. Often, traditional Calvinistic Christians influenced by the historicist eschatology of Reformed theology have applied these warnings to The Roman Catholic, Eastern Orthodox or Liberal Protestant Churches, but not to evangelicals.

A closer reading of the warnings of Jesus and the apostles however make it clear that these false prophets would come among true believers with a mandate from hell to deceive the very elect, in the same way as Israel's false prophets misled Israel (Matthew 7:15, Matthew 24:24, Acts 20:30).

I have been in no doubt that the proliferation of wild deceptions in the church in recent years is being propagated by those very men Paul warned would come in the last times "going from bad to worse, deceiving and being deceived" (2 Timothy 3:13). Neither do I doubt that these trends are preludes to the great "apostasia" or falling away we are told to expect (2 Thessalonians 2:3), paving the way for the ultimate ascendancy of the Man of Lawlessness.

Central to this deception has been a near endless stream of men and women claiming a prophetic office, complete with predictive prophesy, but ignoring that the failure of these predictions made in The Lord's Name is the biblical proof demonstrating them to be false prophets (Deuteronomy 18:20-22). This trend is presently going from bad to worse, and before The Return of Jesus will become worse still. The Restoration Movement, Kingdom Now Reconstructionists, most of the popular Charismatic

Movement, and now much of not only Pentecostalism, but even non-Charismatics influenced by reconstructionism are being more and more given to heeding the voices of those proven to prophesy falsely.

The Word of The Lord assures us that when these deceptions come men who understand will take action and give understanding to the many as the Maccabees did in the days of Antiochus Epiphanes (Daniel 11:33-35).

As is evidenced by his previous two books, I believe my dear friend and brother Bill Randles has been shown by The Lord to be one of those who know their God and take such action. Bill is a pastor with a shepherd's heart for The Lord's sheep. His motive in writing this book has not been unholy anger, profit, self aggrandizement, or jealousy. His motive has been to help protect the Lord's flock, to make other pastors aware of what is going on and to provide them with the material they need to withstand the deceptions that destroy and the wolves that devour.

The church, like Israel, has always had false prophets, but not since the early church have we witnessed as many nor as diverse an array of them as we see today, paraded before us one after another on what represents itself to be Christian TV. While the times are treacherous we can rejoice that Jesus is indeed coming soon. One sign of this is the incredible multiplication of these false prophets deceiving the elect. Another sign of His return however is the rise of those who repel the onslaught at our very gate (Isaiah 28:6).

In view of the urgency of the hour I commend this book to you, that you in turn will be like the Bereans who "examin[ed] the Scriptures daily to see whether these things were so." (Acts 17:11 NASB)

"An appalling and horrible thing
Has happened in the land:
The prophets prophesy falsely,
And the priests rule on their own authority;
And My people love it so!
But what will you do at the end of it?
(Jer 5:30–31 NASB)

4

Chapter One
The Explosion of New Prophets

"I am sending a whole generation of prophets to you. I am about to release prophecy on the church as you have never seen it before... I have a secret plan, and that plan is being unfolded here a little, there a little. Listen to the prophets—the little prophets, the big prophets, listen to those who speak one line and to those who speak volumes... false religion will literally dry up in your day. False religion will go off radio and television. It will lack the funds to continue."
(Prophecy published by the Sweetwater Church of the Valley. Pastor Glenn Foster. Life for the Nations. October 7, 1994).

This book is about the new prophets who seem to have arisen overnight. With their bold personas and even bolder utterances they have captured the imagination of a generation of Christians who, though saved and Spirit filled, seem to have become somehow discontented with simple faith in the scriptures and have hungered for "more." From where do these prophets come? What theological justification do they give for their claims? Most importantly, how do we judge whether they are of God or not? These are some of the questions we seek to answer in this short book. I shall let the prophets speak for themselves as it would be better for you, the reader, to hear from their own words what they believe.

Who am I? No one but a Pentecostal converted in an Assembly of God church and eventually pioneering an independent Pentecostal church in 1982, which I still pastor. Most importantly, I am a Christian, a follower of Jesus Christ. I am concerned, as many other thousands of Christians are, for the purity of the existing church in both doctrine and practice. If these prophets are real, we need them, but if they are false prophets, they pose a threat to the purity, credibility and future integrity of the church. They are especially dangerous to those who are young in the Faith. Let's take a look at these new prophets and their prophecies and teachings.

This advertising in *Charisma* magazine caught my eye, announcing an upcoming "Seers Convocation,"

**INTERNATIONAL SEERS CONVOCATION
EAST MEETS WEST AND SUNRISE MEETS SUNSET
PROPHET E. BERNARD JORDAN
AND PROPHET VERNON ASHE
COMING TOGETHER TO UNVEIL ANCIENT TRUTHS
FOR THE NEW MILLENNIUM TRUTHS THAT WILL HELP
YOU UNLOCK YOUR PROPHETIC ABILITY...**

This full page advertisement in Charisma went on to inform us that, "Prophet Jordan has summoned his newly formed company of prophets to minister to you prophetically. When you register, you'll get your personal appointment with the prophets and a free copy of Bishop Jordan's book, Seeds of Destiny... Before you make another decision in life, let the prophets help you unlock your gift of prophecy."

It should be noted that in Amos 7:12, the word 'Seer' is used derisively, as of someone who has hallucinations, and should not to be taken seriously!

Jordan is far from unique. There are scores of prophets these days from the rapping South African Kim Clement to Rick Joyner and his visions of talking eagles, angelic guided tours of paradise, and conversations with the enthroned departed saints. There is a wide range of the "prophetic" and it is being taken quite seriously by many within the Pentecostal and even Evangelical world. Yes, I said Evangelical. When Evangelicals participate in events such as March for Jesus and Promise Keepers, they are unwittingly involving themselves in both the prophetic and the mystical Spiritual Warfare Movement!

A trip through almost any Christian bookstore would confirm that indeed we are in the midst of a new prophetic movement and it has been steadily increasing for the last ten years. Titles such as *Prophets and Personal Prophecy, The Prophetic Ministry, Apostles, Prophets and the Coming Move of God,* and *Growing in the Prophetic* are among the dozens, even hundreds of titles which have poured out of the Christian presses offering help in dream

6

interpretation, how to develop your prophetic gifting, how to become receptive to the ministry of prophets, even how to compose prophetic songs!!

The new prophets are no longer confined to the margins of popular Christian experience either, they are in influential positions. James Ryle, for example, is the pastor of the Boulder Colorado Vineyard and considers himself a modern-day prophet. He is also the mentor of Bill McCartney, founder of Promise Keepers! In fact, Promise Keepers is seen by many as the fulfillment of the prophecies of Paul Cain and Bob Jones, two "prophets" whom you will meet later. Ryle's book, Hippo in the Garden, was based on a dream he had, which the title describes. One of Ryle's specialties is dream interpretation, and the interpretation of the Hippo Dream was that there would shortly be coming to the church a prophetic movement which will seem as out of place as a hippo in a garden!!

Paul Cain, another of the more prominent prophets is supposed to have gone to George Bush with a prophecy while Bush was in office, and other world leaders have recognized his prophetic gifting, including Saddam Hussein (Yes, THAT Saddam!). Rodney Howard Browne, Bill Hamon, Rick Joyner, Kenneth Copeland and others Who claim to be prophets and who have consistently prophesied that the new prophets would be consulted by world leaders, kings, and heads of nations.

The prophetic movement offers a whole world view, including an interesting prophetic interpretation of the last two decades, the eighties and the nineties. To the prophets, the eighties was the prophetic decade and the nineties is the decade designated as the time for the restoration of the apostles, who are to bring in a "special governmental anointing" which will radically reform the church! Some of these modern prophets say that Christianity will be entirely redefined by these apostles.

"Christ cannot return until His ascension gift ministries have brought the church into full manhood. The Pastor, Evangelist and Teacher have been the only ones acknowledged as being active in that role. But now, Christ is activating His Prophets in the 1980's and His Apostles in the 1990's. Jesus is thrilled at the thought that His prophets will soon be fully recognized by the church."

(Prophets and Personal Prophecy. Bill Hamon. Page 28)

"I believe that the 1980's have been designated in the councils of God as the time for the calling forth of the prophetic ministry. Before the 1980's are over, God will have raised up and called forth thousands of prophets." (Ibid).

Ten thousand to be exact, according to another prophecy. And this new breed of prophets is not in any way cautious about taking to themselves the title of Prophet. This would present no problem as long as there is an intact standard of measurement as Moses described in Deuteronomy 13 and 18.

There are two equally disastrous ditches to avoid however, cessationism and complete gullibility. Cessationism, the erroneous idea that the gifts and ministries of the Holy Spirit have somehow passed away unannounced, is simply indefensible. Many come to this position because of the abuses of the gifts of the Spirit by the ignorant and the self serving! This is unfortunate.

The more common error these days (so it seems) is of those who indiscriminately embrace the complete spectrum of charismatic manifestations. The motives vary, some out of ignorance, others out of a lust for power, and there are those who plunge in, out of a misguided fear of "resisting the move of God." This fear is capitalized upon by the proponents of this movement when they constantly refer to Ananias and Sapphira, or to being left in the dust as the "advancing church" moves on with God! "Touch not my anointed and do my prophets no harm," is one of the more commonly abused scriptures, being used to bludgeon critical thinking.

Of course, we do not have to choose between total abandon and dead, dry religion. Those are not the only two options! The neo-gnostics do not have a monopoly on experiential religion and those who want to faithfully discern are not "religious deadheads!" It is our emphatic contention that Christianity is both experiential and at the same time is the "thinking man's religion!" We can be both Pentecostal and Berean! The Bereans were considered noble because they were not blindly accepting what the Apostle Paul said, but sought the scriptures "to see if these things be so." In the New Testament there are two verses that keep these two aspects (the experiential and the analytical) in healthy tension. 1 Thessalonians 5:20-21 teaches us to "Despise not prophesying" on the one hand, yet at the same time, to "Prove [test] all things and hold fast to that which is good." 1 Corinthians 14:40 admonishes us to "Let everything be done" (including, from the context, the gifts of tongues, interpretation, and prophecy) while at the same time "decently and in order" which is going to require some discriminate thinking.

It is this kind of thinking which is currently being strangled to death as often as possible by the new, bold, manipulative "prophets" and "apostles" whose constant mantra is something to the effect of "God is so much bigger than His Word" or "God is offending our minds so that He can reach our hearts," and of course one of the more manipulative, "Most Christians have more faith in Satan's ability to deceive us than in God's ability to bless us." This is starkly contrasted to God's own perspective which is expressed by David, who praises God for the fact that He "Has magnified His Word even above His Name!"

The effect of this steady beat has been to disarm the believer's ability to make the critical judgements needed to "Be sober, be vigilant, for your adversary the devil walks about as a roaring lion." At a time when sobriety is desperately needed, spiritual drunkenness is being promoted to the unwary, and they are being seduced by the idea that as the great Last Days overcomers, ("cutting edge Christians," the "manchild company") discernment is the last thing they need to be concerned about. Perhaps we can yet rouse some to "Buy the truth and sell it not," and awaken others out of their drunken slumber, "redeeming the time, for the days are evil". If God should grant us repentance, there will still be time to recover ourselves out of the snare of the Devil, and many of our brothers and sisters will believe and acknowledge the truth. That is the purpose of this book. May God bless you through this writing as we look at the new prophets.

Chapter 2
The Theology of the New Prophets

"God's people are going to start to exercise rule, and they're going to take dominion over the power of Satan. They're going to bring diabolical princes down. The dark powers that hover over the parliament buildings of the nations are going to be paralyzed by the corporate prayer of an authoritative community. As the rod of His strength goes out of Zion, He'll change legislation. He'll chase the devil off the face of God's earth, and God's people together, doing the will of God, will bring about God's purposes and God's reign."
(Ern Baxter. National Men's Shepherds Conference. Kansas City, Missouri. Sept. 1975)

The only way to understand the teachings and utterances of the new prophets is to look at the underlying theological framework that has informed most of them. The prophetic movement has come out of the Pentecostal world and particularly the late 1940's revival called the New Order of the Latter Rain. From the Latter Rain movement came the Manifested Sons of God heresy, which was renounced by the Assemblies of God in 1949. Though it was discredited, its ideals have taken on a heretical life of their own, they have resurfaced under a different name and have been promoted by various personalities.

The Pentecostal revival exploded on the world at the turn of the century in a blaze of fire, sweeping millions into the Kingdom of God, and it happened spontaneously all over the world. People from all walks of life were touched by the revival, but especially the disenfranchised. Certainly there were problems, for the revival was composed mainly of the uneducated and disenfranchised, therefore there are testimonies of erroneous teaching and extreme practices. However, at least the early Pentecostal leaders were Christ centered, willing to adjust their doctrine as they learned scripture.

What they lacked in education, they made up for in sincerity and Christ centeredness. Thus, millions had been touched and transformed by the Pentecostal revival! But, by the 1930's and 1940's, many were wondering where the fire had gone. It seemed as if the churches had settled into the very complacency that the first generation Pentecostal pioneers had once criticized in the main line churches. That second generation of Pentecostals, raised on stories of "what it was like when the fire fell," began to feel like the generation in Judges 2, who "knew not the mighty works of the Lord."

But, the post World War Two period seemed to bring with it a breath of fresh air, not only for Pentecostals, but Evangelicals also. A virtual explosion of evangelists came on the scene, and before long, names such as A.A. Allen, T.L. Osborn, Oral Roberts, and Jack Coe became household words. These evangelists emphasized salvation and divine healing, and were very innovative in the use of the media. Radio and eventually television became the means of expansion to many Pentecostal ministries, and gradually the expectation began to change for many Pentecostals. The old line Pentecostals had a simple message, for the most part, "Jesus saves, Jesus heals, Jesus baptizes in the Holy Spirit, and Jesus is coming again." They also stressed the "power of the blood," of Jesus and the hope of Jesus' soon return. It permeates the hymnody, for example, songs like "I'll Fly Away," "Changed in the Twinkling of an Eye," "We Shall See the King," and so forth. The early Pentecostals held no stock in this world, they longed for the dawning of the coming new day, inaugurated at the coming of the Lord Jesus. Unlike their current pneumo-centric (spirit centered) offspring, the early Pentecostals were passionately Christocentric! But, with the new found success, and the seeming power of the new evangelists, preachers and teachers began to talk about the "new thing" that God was going to be doing.

What do we mean, "new thing?" It comes from Isaiah 43:19, "Behold I do a new thing; now it shall spring forth; shall you not know it?" According to sound principles of *hermeneutics* (biblical interpretation), the new thing which God promised to Israel is contrasted to the old thing which they had already been experiencing. But, according to the new teachers, the new thing is still to come, a "Great Last Days Revival," that will supposedly sweep the world for Jesus, bringing whole nations into the Kingdom. Thus gradually, instead of looking for the bodily return of Jesus, the focus was switched to the day when we would come into our own great power and glory, the "new thing." This explains why Christians who have been saved by Jesus and filled with the Holy Spirit are willing to jump on planes, charter buses, and travel great distances upon the report of a possible outbreak of the "new thing." This is not recent either, it goes back further than Toronto and Pensacola. People have been seeking this "new thing" for at least fifty years!

Another similarly misinterpreted scriptural concept is the Latter Rain. Hosea 6:3, Joel 2:23, and James 5:7 speak of the latter rain. Once again, hermeneutics comes into play. The "former and latter rain" refer allegorically to the agricultural calendar of the land of Israel. The former rain, which was vital to the preparation for planting season, corresponds to the law of Moses. It does to people's hearts what the plowing does to the ground, it breaks up the hardness, convicting of sin. "The law of the Lord is perfect, converting the soul." Psalm 19. The latter rains in Israel are essential for the perfecting of the crop for harvest. This corresponds to the giving of the Spirit on Pentecost. It is the Spirit who prepares hearts to be harvested for Jesus, and who gives life. Interestingly enough, both the giving of the law and the sending of the Spirit took place on the Feast of Pentecost. The number 3000 is also involved in both of these, for after the giving of the law, Israel rebelled and 3000 were slain. After the giving of the Spirit, Peter preached and 3000 were saved. "The letter kills, but the Spirit gives life." But, like the new thing, the Latter Rain concept evolved into an expectation of something other than the indelling of the Spirit, a coming "outpouring." The Former Rain was now interpreted as Pentecost, or even Azusa Street, but something even greater was about to break forth. Rather than proclaiming the hoped for Parousia, the bodily Return of Jesus, the preaching and prophecies began to focus on the things we would be doing in the "next great revival." The actual coming of Jesus as an imminent reality was actually taught by some to be an impossibility, on the grounds that the church had not yet restored "all things." Where did they get this idea? From another badly distorted scripture, Acts 3:20-21.

And He shall send Jesus Christ, which before was preached unto you: Whom the heaven must receive until the time of restitution of all things, which God hath spoken by the mouth of all His holy prophets since the world began.

The context for this scripture, hermeneutically, is the Temple, addressed to the Jews, who were awaiting their Messiah, the one whom they believed would restore the Davidic fortunes of Israel. Peter points to the restoration of the cripple in the name of Jesus, and proclaims that it attests to the fact that the Messiah they awaited, was the one that they failed to recognize and had crucified and slain. This one whom they had rejected, God has vindicated by the resurrection of Jesus, and upon Israel's repentance, Jesus will be sent back to them, at the times of the "restoration of all things." (The fortunes of Israel). It is another way of saying what Jesus said on his last speech in the temple, "Behold your house is left unto you desolate. For I say unto you, ye shall not see me henceforth, until ye shall say, 'Blessed is he that comes in the name of the Lord.'" (Matthew 23:38-39). The other place and context of that word "restore" is in the first chapter of Acts, verse 6, where the apostles ask, "Lord, will you at this time restore the kingdom to Israel?" Note that the Lord would have had an excellent opportunity to give them the correct meaning of the restoration of all things, supposedly as applying to the "restoration" of the church, and not Israel, but He didn't. The apostles were right. Restoration, both New Testament and Old, applies to Israel, not the church.

However, the interpretation of Acts 3:20-21 has evolved along with Isaiah 43 and the passages that speak of the latter rain. Instead of Israel (and the church) awaiting the times of restoration of all things, (which the Father hath put in His own power, Acts 1:7), the new interpretation is that it is now the Father and Jesus Christ, who are waiting for we, the church, to complete its own restoration! For example, Earl Paulk states in his book, *The Wounded Body of Christ*, that we the church,

> "Have been foreordained of God to become that people who will become so glorified that we can bring Christ back to the earth. This glorified church must make the earth God's footstool before Jesus can come again."
>
> *(From **The Wounded Body of Christ**. Earl Paulk, as quoted in Jewel van der Merwe's book **Joel's Army**).*

13

Paulk states as plain as any, Jesus can't come back until *we* get it together. He is supposedly "held in the heavens" awaiting the church to restore all things. In this view, before the church can restore anything else, she must be restored herself, having lost the glory and power God intended to have her to walk in, down through the Ages. Supposedly, now, the church is doing it, we are in continuous restoration, starting with Luther, who restored Justification of Faith, then Wesley restored Sanctification, Dowie divine healing, and Azusa Street the Baptism of the Holy Ghost and speaking in tongues. According to the restorationist world view, the church is progressing, as other facets of Christianity are being restored. But there is much more to come before Jesus can return! Lately, spiritual warfare, deliverance, prayer marching, open churches, Davidic worship, and of primary importance, the restoration of the "five-fold ministry" especially the last two offices, the apostle and the prophet. It is believed that under the "apostolic and prophetic" anointings that the church will finally perfect herself, and become a "glorious church, without spot or wrinkle" and built upon the foundation of the (new) apostles and prophets, of course, Christ Jesus being the chief cornerstone.

These were the presuppositions that were swirling around the Pentecostal world in the late 1940's, supplanting the other-worldly hope of the Parousia, the bodily return of Jesus. Powerful and well received sign gift ministries such as that of William Branham (whom I will speak of in the next chapter), Jack Coe, A.A. Allen, and Oral Roberts seemed to herald the dawn of a new day of power and anointing just around the corner. Another influence in Pentecostal circles, was a little book called *Atomic Power with God Through Prayer and Fasting*, which purported to teach the secret of immortality and increased anointing through extended fasting. The popularity of that book attests to the hunger for power that had developed in the churches.

In the late 1940's, ironically, at another "airport fellowship" in Canada, at a combination Bible school, orphanage, and church called the Sharon Home, George Hawtin and Percy Hunt, both heavily influenced by both Branham and the book, *Atomic Power with God Through Prayer and Fasting*, began praying and preaching a coming Latter Rain. After a season of united prayer and fasting at the Bible school, a prophecy came forth in one of the classes. It, in effect, proclaimed the beginning of the new thing. That God would restore to the church the gifts of the Spirit and ministries of the apostles and the prophet, and that gifts and ministries would be "imparted" by the laying on of hands by those vessels whom God would so designate. Classes were canceled, the prayer meeting was extended, the word leaked out, and crowds began to gather. By that summer, thousands from all over the world had gathered for a camp meeting in Saskatchewan, Canada seeking the new anointing. This was the genesis of what became known as the Latter Rain Revival. William Menzies, who wrote the official history of the Assemblies of God, *Anointed to Serve* summarized the new thing this way,

> "In 1947, George Hawtin and Percy Hunt launched an independent Bible school in North Battleford, Saskatchewan... They evolved a teaching that emphasized extreme congregationalism with local authority committed to a restored order of apostles having received a special dispensation derived through the laying on of hands, could in turn dispense a variety of spiritual gifts. Their extravagant claims and their belligerent attack on existing Pentecostal groups brought open conflict. Many sincere Christians followed the new group, which boasted of being a fresh revival displacing the apostatized Pentecostals."
> **(*Anointed To Serve*. *Gospel Publishing House. William Menzies*).**

The characteristics Menzies outlined are interesting because the issues of "impartation," personal prophecies, restored apostles and prophets, belligerent attacks on existing Pentecostals, and extravagant claims have been the consistent pattern ever since the late 1940's. Impartation of anointing is what we are seeing currently, in both the Toronto and Pensacola revivals, where people are literally embarking on pilgrimages in the hopes of receiving "the anointing." Belligerent attacks on existing Pentecostals, can still be seen by those constant references to the established church, as being "Jezebel," "Saul," dead religion, "the accuser of the brethren." As in the late 1940's, a good many Pentecostal churches have been broken up as the new apostles and prophets seek to draw disciples after themselves after downgrading the leadership of the established churches. You might notice that the new breed

of prophets and apostles never seem to miss an opportunity to mock and castigate "religious deadheads," Jezebel spirits," "Old Order" people, all of which are
the names they use to refer to those who dare question the orthodoxy of practices such as "holy laughter," spiritual drunkenness, and other such manifestations. As for "extravagant claims" as Menzies called them, there have been
many. We are the generation, supposedly, in which "all of the purposes of God
are wrapped up in," the believers will walk in "unprecedented levels of power
and authority," whole nations will "tremble at the mention of their [new apostles and prophets] names," and these new prophets will be sought out by the
"Presidents, the pharaohs, and the Babylonian emperors of this world." One of
our current new prophets has been shown that in the end they will be saying (of
us) "He [God] saved the best for last."

Menzies' quote gives us the Assemblies of God view (at the time of
this book) of the Latter Rain. J. Preston Eby, a Latter Rain teacher gives a
more favorable view of the movement,

"In 1948, the very year Israel became a nation, another great
deluge fell from heaven, a mighty revival called "The Latter
Rain." In this restoration revival, God did a work which far
transcended the... Pentecostal outpouring of forty years before.
All nine gifts of the spirit, the fivefold ministries of apostles,
prophets, evangelists, pastors, and teachers, spiritual praise and
worship, and end-time revelation of God's purpose to Manifest
His Sons, a glorious church, to bring in the Kingdom of God,
all of this and much more was restored among God's people."

The phrase "Manifested Sons of God", which Eby referred to, comes
from Romans 8:19, and the "revelation" which Eby referred to, became the
name of a submovement which sprang out of the Latter Rain. "For the
earnest expectation of the creation waiteth for the manifestation of the sons
of God," has long been interpreted as referring to the bodily return of Jesus
Christ, to reverse the "curse of futility" imposed on the creation by God at
the fall. At his coming, the lion will lay down with the lamb, and the meek
(the sons of God, the believers) will be glorified for all to see.

16

In the "revelation of sonship," Romans 8:19 is seen as something that an elite company of believers attains to, through progressive revelation of "who we are in Christ." All of this sin-cursed creation awaits not the Parousia, but the coming into a glorification of an elite remnant of Christians! These Manifested Sons are glorified through progressive revelation of their "sonship." The Manifested Sons are seen as Christ. In this error the identity of Jesus Christ and the identity of the Body of Christ, the church, are confused. Some MSOG teachers even refer to an "ongoing incarnation of Christ," and imply that Christ has to come within us before He can ever come unto us. Prerogatives and responsibilities assigned to the resurrected Lord Jesus Christ alone have been assumed by those who have believed this error.

> "At that time the sons of God will be fully manifested on the earth. Widespread spiritual warfare will result with the sons of God doing battle with Satan and company, the non-Christian nations of this world will also be defeated. Once the earth has been subdued, Jesus will come back to earth and be given the Kingdom that has been won for Him by this "manchild company." The Manifested Sons of God doctrine teaches that these sons will be equal to Jesus Christ: immortal, sinless, perfected sons who have partaken of the divine nature. They will have every right to be called gods and will be called gods."
> **(Prophets and the Prophetic Movement. Bill Hamon).**

What a perversion of I Corinthians 15:24-28! It is HE, Jesus, who will "put down all rule and authority and power," and HE also, who must "Put all enemies under His feet," and HE who after accomplishing all of this himself, will turn it all over to the Father, that "God will be all in all." HE is Jesus, not we the church. You can see, very quickly, the confusion of these two identities, and that confusion has begin to permeate the church.

Supposedly, the Manifested Sons of God will even be able, without the bodily return of Christ, to overcome even death! Paulk again, states,

> "The last enemy to be conquered is death. Who will conquer it? A mature church will come forth, with the kind of authority

and power that will be able to stand in the very face of Satan. When the church reaches that level of maturity, God will be able to say, 'This generation of the church does not need to die. She has reached the place of maturity, I will translate her because her maturity pleases me.' "

(*The Eternal Church.* Paulk)

Not all of the church, mind you, but the elite remnant, also known as either the Overcomers, the Manchild, the Joseph Company, and so forth. This whole movement appeals to elitism, the desire to be distinct, as Jude said, "These be they who separate themselves." For years the people of God have been steadily conditioned to think in terms of levels, "30 fold Christians, 60 and 100 fold saints," or "outer court, inner court, and holy of holies Christians." There is the "traditional church" as opposed to "the Manchild company," "the bride company," the "advancing church," "the prophetic church" and so forth. This, in a nutshell, is the flattering heresy permeating the Pentecostal and evangelical world, the idea that without the Parousia we can perfect ourselves into the "greatest expression of the church ever seen."

Besides the ongoing revelation, and the ministries of apostles and prophets, the only other way of being "glorified" and brought into full "sonship" is through impartations of the presence of God. It is this "presence" that many are seeking in their pilgrimages to various cities. God is, supposedly, "incarnating His Church." It is also known as the Glory, or the New Anointing. Many who have been to Toronto, Pensacola, Anaheim Vineyard, Rick Joyner meetings and other venues, have seen this "glory" as a silver cloud or at times as a blueish haze, Jude again, "These be they who separate themselves, they are sensual." (v19)

This new anointing is what has spawned a host of chartered buses, pilgrimages little different than the Catholic pilgrimages to Lourdes and other Marion sites. Rather than waiting patiently for the Parousia of our Lord Jesus Christ, who alone will undo the curse on this earth and glorify his saints, these neo-gnostics cherish a different hope, their own attainment of glorification. The church herself presenting the earth which she has conquered, unto Jesus. Also an anointing (Christ) that has not come unto us in the flesh, but that gets us drunk, gives us visions and ultimately, deifies us.

18

As one friend of mine put it, after "seeking the new anointing" as far back as 1960, she and her husband tired of "chasing the Charismatic carrot on a stick," and accepted the glorious realization that all we have needed has been given unto us in Christ, and it is in Him that we are to put our hope. This "revival" is nothing new. There are many who have for years been listening to the same kind of prophecies, and been just as willing as anyone else to run to the next meeting, seeking the "new thing" or "more" from the Lord, believing the Great Revival is just around the corner.

This is a brief overview of the theology of the new prophetic movement. Others have done a more thorough treatment of it. I'm thinking of Al Dager's book, *Vengeance is Ours*, (Sword Publishing. PO Box 290, Redmond, WA, 98073-0290) which gives a more thorough treatment of the doctrine and its implications. In the 1940's, instead of imminent glory, the Latter Rain/Manifested Sons of God was reproached. The Assemblies of God repudiated the doctrine and practices, and the movement went into a forty year wilderness (as they see it). It would not entirely die out. The basic doctrines went forth under different names and through other vessels. Alternately, the Neo-Pentecostal Movement, the Word of Faith, Dominionism, Kingdom Now, The Sonship Message, The Walk, Shepherding and Accountability, Restorationism, and much of the Charismatic movement were used as vessels of the doctrines and teachings of this heresy down through the last forty years. It would not be until the late 1980's that the leavening had caused the MSOG doctrine to flower forth in full expression, through the Kansas City Prophets, Paul Cain, and the Vineyard Movement. For many, the one hope that the false concept of "sonship" was valid, was in the memory of an archetypical "son" who it seemed to have worked for, William Branham. In order to further understand the new prophetic movement, one must consider his unusual story.

Chapter Three

The Model Prophet

A little boy in the hills of Kentucky is sorely disappointed for his friends were all playing ball, but his daddy had told him to "pack water" for the family. As he toted the heavy buckets, he heard a sound in the top of a poplar tree like the sound of a whirlwind, which was strange, for there was no breeze evident anywhere else. But strange occurrences were nothing new to this little boy, his whole life seemed to be marked by them. Suddenly, he heard an audible voice which instructed him, "Don't you ever drink, smoke or defile your body in any way. There will be work for you when you are older." Although this frightened little William Branham, it was only one of a number of remarkable occurrences in the life of this poor and uneducated Kentucky boy. Even at his birth it was reported that,

> "A light come whirling through the window, about the size of a pillow, and circled around where I was and went down on the bed."
> **(Footprints on the Sands of Time**, the Autobiography of William Branham)

The friends and neighbors who witnessed the sight were awestruck. Gordon Lindsay, who also wrote a biography of William Branham, begins in this fashion,

> "The story of the life of William Branham is so out of this world and beyond the ordinary that were there not available a host of infallible proofs which document and attest its authenticity, one might well be excused for considering it farfetched and incredible. But the facts are so generally known, and of such a

nature that they can easily be verified by any sincere investigator, that they stand as God's witness to His willingness and purpose to reveal Himself again to men as He once did in the days of the prophets and the apostles. The story of this prophet's life-for he is a Prophet...indeed witnesses to the fact that Bible days are here again."

*(William Branham, **A Man Sent From God**, by Gordon Lindsay)*

Wow! This man left quite an impression on the people of his time! This introduction to Lindsay's book reads like the introduction to the Gospel of Luke! Branham still leaves an impression, even on a new generation. Paul Cain, Bob Jones, Rodney Howard Browne, Kenneth Copeland, Kenneth Hagin and many other current leaders in the Charismatic movement speak extremely highly of Branham, in many cases as a true and great prophet of God. He is credited with being the father of the Latter Rain Revival, his teachings led to the Manifested Sons of God teaching, the Word of Faith teaching, and for our present purposes, the current prophetic movement owes much to the influence of this man.

Who is William Branham and why is he important to our discussion? As stated earlier, Branham's whole life was marked by a series of supernatural or paranormal experiences from his birth. As he put it one time,

"There was always that peculiar feeling, like someone standing near me, trying to say something to me, and especially when I was alone. No one seemed to understand me at all."

*(From Branham's message, **"How the Gift Came"**)*

Even as an unconverted teenager, Branham's purity was safeguarded, for at critical moments of temptation, he would hear the sound of the whirling breeze and remember the instructions of the "voice." Eventually, Branham married, was converted, and even became a Baptist minister. At a public baptism administered by Branham, 4000 people witnessed a light shining down on Branham and some heard the voice tell him that he would be as John the Baptist, a forerunner of the second coming of Christ. Many who witnessed this ran in fear and many worshiped! Eventually when Branham was about 40, he had a crisis experience in which he fasted and prayed and sought the answer to the "presence" and the "voice" which had accompanied him all his life. After some hours in a cabin out in the woods, Branham relates,

> "Then along in the night, at about the eleventh hour, I had quit praying and was sitting up when I noticed a light flickering in the room. Thinking someone was coming with a flashlight, I looked out the window, but there was no one, and when I looked back, the light was spreading out on the floor and getting wider...as I looked up there hung that great star...it looked more like a ball of fire or light shining down upon the floor...coming through the light, I saw the feet of a man coming toward me...He appeared to be a man who, in human weight would weigh about two hundred pounds, clothed in a white robe. He had a smooth face, no beard, dark hair down to his shoulders, rather dark complected with a very pleasant countenance...Seeing how fearful I was he said, "FEAR NOT. I AM SENT FROM THE PRESENCE OF ALMIGHTY GOD TO TELL YOU THAT YOUR PECULIAR LIFE AND YOUR MISUNDERSTOOD WAYS HAVE BEEN TO INDICATE THAT GOD HAS SENT YOU TO TAKE A GIFT OF DIVINE HEALING TO THE PEOPLE OF THE WORLD. IF YOU WILL BE SINCERE AND CAN GET THE PEOPLE TO BELIEVE YOU, NOTHING SHALL STAND BEFORE YOUR PRAYERS, NOT EVEN CANCER."
>
> *(Lindsay's book, **Branham**. Page 77).*

The angel went on to proclaim unto him the twofold gifting ordained for Branham,

> "One of them will be that you will take the person that you are praying for by the hand with your left hand and their right, then just stand quiet and...there'll be a physical effect that'll happen on your body...then you pray, and if it leaves, the disease is gone from the people. If it doesn't leave then just ask a blessing and walk away."

The other sign given would be that it would be given to Branham to know the "secrets of men's hearts." The angel also promised Branham that, "I will be with you and the gift will grow greater and greater."

Branham went on to catapult from almost complete obscurity to international fame by holding whole auditoriums and even stadiums spellbound through the exercise of these two "sign gifts." This ministry, along with an explosion of other healing evangelists, was to give the Pentecostal Movement a tremendous boost in the 1940's and 1950's. But there was one problem with Branham's ministry, the teaching.

Branham was discouraged from teaching by many in the Pentecostal Movement, "Just stick with the signs and wonders, the words of knowledge and the healings." Why? As soon as Branham began to share what he actually believed, it made many people nervous. For example, Branham believed the doctrine known as the "Serpent's Seed" teaching. This heresy teaches that the Fall came about when Eve commenced a sexual relationship with Lucifer, thus putting the blame on woman. Out of that illicit union, was born Cain, and through his descent has come the "wicked" which are with us to this day. Branham also propagated the heretical "Oneness views" and even stated that the doctrine of the Trinity was "of the devil!" He believed in the dispensational view of the seven churches of the book of Revelation, that these are seven epochs in church history, but his twist to this was that he was the Angel (Messenger) of the seventh church, Laodicea. He prophesied that the Rapture would occur in 1977, and taught that the Bible, the Zodiac, and the Egyptian pyramids were all forms of the Word of God. (William Branham, *Adoption*. Jeffersonville, Indiana. Spoken Word Publications). When asked if it was the Holy Spirit that performed his many signs and wonders, Branham replied, "NO, I do them by my Angel." In truth, by his own admission, Branham was as helpless as a baby without his angel. Branham denied an eternal Hell and taught that denominationalism was the mark of the beast. The Word of Faith teaching, that reality can be created by the spoken Word, and the basic teaching of the Manifested Sons of God, both have their beginnings in the teachings of Branham.

There is so much more I could say about this remarkable man, who had such a widespread impact on the Pentecostal and Charismatic world.

Branham, on several occasions, was seen by even hostile witnesses to have a halo!! There are two photos, one taken by a hostile photographer hired by a man bent on exposing Branham as a false prophet, which when developed showed a halo over his head. This photo, reproduced in Gordon Lindsay's book, also has a certified letter from an investigator of questionable documents assuring the public that nothing had been done to tamper with the film! How do you question a man with a halo?

Not everyone accepted Branham as a prophet of God. Kurt Koch, a respected evangelical scholar who specialized in the study of the occult and demon possession, featured Branham in his book, *Between Christ and Satan,* where he wrote,

"The question of discernment is of great importance, especially in the field of miracles. There are some miracle healers whose work is so hard to evaluate that Christians are often in doubt as to the forces behind these people. We have today for example men such as Tommy Hicks, Harry Edwards, T. L. Osborn and William Branham. Each one of these men depends on mass meetings which are followed by a call to people to step forward for healing. I have, over the years, collected a lot of information on these particular people and the conclusions that I have come to are not based on a superficial judgement of the matter...I have compared their teachings with the Holy Scriptures. My aim is to obey the plain meaning of the Bible, which tells us to "Try the spirits, to see whether they are from God"...the man who poses us with the most problems is Branham. He not only exhibits abilities of fortune telling, mesmerism, and magic, but he also has certain Christian characteristics. His whole work is hidden behind a screen of Christian words and phrases. Both his parents believed in fortune telling and he was burdened with occultism at an early age. He once told an audience...that he had visionary experiences since childhood...My comment is that the gifts of the Spirit are not imparted to a person at birth, but they receive them after their spiritual rebirth."

Koch relates an example of the gift in operation in Zurich,

"He called a young man to the platform. He then asked the young man, 'Do we know each other?' 'No,' was the reply. Branham went on to say, 'Have you got a letter in your pocket from a young lady?' this time the answer was, 'Yes.' 'There is a picture with the letter.' 'That's right.' 'Will you show me the picture?' The young man pulled it out and Branham held it out for all...to see. 'Am I not a prophet?' he called out. There was an enthusiastic response from the people together with cries of 'Hallelujah' and 'Praise the Lord!' But we ask, is a piece of fortune telling proof of ones prophetic ability? There should be no confusion here, as the Bible points out, fortune telling is of the devil (Acts 16:16)."

(Between Christ and Satan. Kurt Koch).

Branham died suddenly in a head on auto collision in 1965, yet his followers were so sure that he would rise from the dead, they put off burying him for quite some time! In 1961, the Full Gospel Businessmen's Association's Voice magazine said this of Branham,

"In Bible days, there were men of God who were prophets and seers, but in all the sacred records, none of these had a greater ministry than that of William Branham."

The Word of Faith Movement, the Manifested Sons of God, and the current Prophetic movement are all part of the legacy and influence of this one man, William Branham. Though he was eventually regarded with suspicion because of his erratic teachings, many have been enamored and directly influenced by him, who are now influencing hundreds of thousands of this generation who don't really know anything but good about William Branham. After all, he had the power, didn't he? As Al Dager says in his excellent book, *Vengeance is Ours,*

"William Branham's body is still in the grave. But his occult methodology of healing was picked up by hundreds of pastors and teachers upon whom he laid his hands and who have traded on it to a greater or lesser degree."

25

Chapter Four

The Decade of the Prophets

"The eighties revealed my prophets you see, and the nineties revealed my government and my justice, even improving on this day...And yes my good shepherds that are coming out of many places, they will put to rest the troubled waters in the church...They will have authority to speak against those that lie, the gossips, the slanderers, those that trouble the waters..."
(Excerpt from a forty five minute prophecy given by Bob Jones[1])

As we have looked at earlier, in the theology of the Latter Rain/Manifested Sons of God, the church cannot come into her glory until the prophetic and apostolic anointings are restored, for it is they who will come on the scene to bring divine order and authority to the church. As one prominent prophetic leader has declared,

"The company of prophets will help restore the apostles back into their rightful place in the church. The full restoration of apostles and prophets back into the church will bring divine order, unity, purity, and maturity to the corporate Body of Christ."

(Bill Hamon)

In the late 1980's, the "prophetic" seemed to begin breaking forth, and not on an isolated scale, either. A Pentecostal church in Kansas City, known simply at that time as the Kansas City Fellowship, became world renowned as a laboratory for the development of the prophetic ministry. It was centered around a band of men who were to become known as the Kansas City Prophets. The young, earnest, pastor, Mike Bickle had, on a trip to Cairo, Egypt, heard an audible voice tell him,

"I am inviting you to raise up a work that will touch the ends of the earth. I have invited many people to do this thing and many people have said yes, but very few have done my will."

The "work" that Bickle had been invited to raise up, was a seven faceted amalgamation of various traveling prophetic and apostolic ministries dedicated to church planting and intercession. The seven facets were: apostolic teams, city churches, the House of Prayer, the Joseph Company, the Israel Mandate, a ministry training center, and Shiloh ministries, which was a type of retreat and training center bringing novice and experienced prophets together for ministry.

Before long, Kansas City Fellowship had become internationally known as a prophetic center. Bickle had surrounded himself with a band of prophets who, for the most part, taught and prophesied the old Manifested Sons themes. An outstanding example of this is found in the tapes from the church entitled, "Visions and Revelations," which were soon distributed across the English speaking world. The tapes consist of Bickle interviewing prophet Bob Jones. Bickle draws out of Jones his testimonies of countless mystical experiences, dreams, visions, revelations and demonic attacks on his person. Peretti could write a book on this guy! For example,

[Mike Bickle] " You know, I'm going to tell you something about Bob [Jones]. Ever since that time he was filled with the Holy Spirit in '74 he began to see technicolor visions and the Lord began to visit him...He has five or ten visions and dreams a night!"

There is a lingo, that one must adopt to understand the terms and concepts of the prophets, and it is the terminology of the Latter Rain/Manifested Sons of God. It constantly speaks of "birthing" and bringing forth the bride. It assumes personalities such as Jezebel and Elijah, are currently in conflict (spiritually, allegorically). In this view, the manchild of Revelation 12 has yet to come forth and, as is the case with all gnostics, soon the symbolic assumes more reality than the real. From the same tape, Jones holds forth,

[Bob Jones] "The Last Days church is being birthed out of the old church, and the old leadership is coming to an end and the new, young leadership is being raised up to reign over an end time church that will bring forth the bride."

Sounds good, but what did he say? One would have to be conditioned to think allegorically in order to understand this. It goes back to the Latter Rain attacks on the existing church that Menzies wrote of. "The Old Church," in this thinking, is like Saul. And Jones prophesies that the "Old Leadership" is coming to an end to make room for the new, a kind of Saul and David scenario. In this prophecy, one also learns that the Bride hasn't even "come forth" yet. This is an example of the elite concept: not all Christians qualify to be the Bride, nor the saints down through time, for the Bride supposedly is to be "birthed" in the Last Days Church. The worldwide appeal of this tape is mystifying. It could only be a spiritual phenomenon that so many in the Pentecostal and Charismatic churches (not to mention the many evangelicals) were enamored by this tape.

Jones, supposedly, has a standing appointment with the Lord, for on the Day of Atonement, the Lord comes to "stand before" Jones yearly. Also, Jones inaugurated an annual day of judgement in the church described in another Jones/Bickle interview, entitled "The Shepherd's Rod." At this day, Bickle and the whole church passed under the prophet's shepherd's rod for an annual inspection of the fruit of their lives! Is any of this based on the teachings of the apostles as normative standards of Christianity? Did the apostles have personal annual appointments with Jesus, on holy feast days? This is Jones' personal gnosis, private revelation knowledge that he claims came to him, obviously unmediated. In other words, he is a gnostic, who has broken into some mystical experiences, and been accepted as a prophet of God!

We are told by one who could actually boast of some really valid spiritual experiences that, "No prophecy of scripture is of private interpretation." The one who was actually on the Mount of Transfiguration with Jesus, Moses, and Elijah would turn us to the "More sure word of prophecy...(scripture)," and "to beware of the false teachers among you...who secretly lay truth alongside of error...[literal Greek, para soxouisan]." (See 2

28

Peter 1:16-2:2). Yes, there is indeed a Day of Atonement, but no, Jones doesn't have an actual standing appointment with the Lord of Glory, annually on that day!

Earlier, Menzies also spoke of the "extravagant claims" of the Latter Rain proponents, which are echoed in the Bickle/Jones tapes,

[Mike Bickle] "He [God] said, 'I'll cause 300,000 to bear a distinct anointing over the one billion [converts]...They will have a special measure of the Spirit...there is one generation that will enter into that beyond all others. The chosen generation of history that will go beyond all others in power.' "

[Bob Jones] "From out of the sands of time I [God] have called the best of every bloodline in the earth unto this generation...Even the bloodline of Paul. Even the bloodline of David, the bloodline of Peter, James, and John. The best of their seed is unto this generation. They will even be superior to them in heart, stature, and love for me."

It never ceases to amaze me that such blatant error was overlooked by the thousands of those who so eagerly embraced the Kansas City Prophets. The anticipation for the "new thing," the Latter Rain, Great Last Days Revival, that the Manifested Sons of God, Charismatic, and Word of Faith teachers had conditioned so many for, has effectively blinded us. When the word spread that there were "prophets" in the land, Kansas City became in the 1980's what North Battleford, Canada was in the summer of 1948, what Toronto became in 1994, and Pensacola has become in these days. The mecca of thousands from around the world who are seeking the new anointing. Among the many who came to behold were John Wimber and Paul Cain. Wimber, as the head of the Vineyard Movement, quickly became enamored by the prophets and embraced their ministry, giving them further worldwide exposure. Another who was drawn to their light was Paul Cain, also a prophet and a former associate minister to William Branham, who had retired from public prophetic ministry after being disillusioned by the greed he saw there. He had felt called by God to leave the limelight to enter a simple life, "marked by bible study and prayer."

Jones and Bickle, in their widely distributed interviews, whetted an appetite in many for mystical experiences, which Jones abounds in. Including the appearance of a spirit named Dominus who, according to Jones, is Jesus; also his encounters with a talking white horse; and demonic attacks which left gashes on his arms. As Bickle explained,

> "Bob Jones has come to me several times after ministry...you may not believe this ...where he went to bed at night and woke up in the morning with a big red streak across his face or a big cut, a gash, on his arm. He'd say, 'They got me last night,' he was at warfare in the realm of trances and visions and there was marks left on his body."

Jones could even tell Bickle what dreams he was going to have, as well as come to him in his dreams! Like Branham, Jones confesses to being burdened with the paranormal at an early age. Once, Jones was hit by lightening and out of that experience he developed "Golden Senses," the ability to feel in his hands and arms sensations that would signal various spiritual realities,

> [Mike Bickle] "Bob...we talked about the golden senses because you said that the Lord is going to be...touching the senses...the Lord visited Bob, I think in '75 and touched him by the Spirit of God...the phrase Bob uses is his senses turn golden, that means his five physical senses literally were inspired by the Holy Spirit...He could tell what was happening in the Spirit realm...there's twenty or thirty different signs that show up in his body."

This is the kind of thing which drew literally thousands of seekers to Kansas City and inaugurated the 1980's as the prophetic decade.

Paul Cain, whom we made reference to earlier, as a young man in the 1940's and 1950's, was a rising star in the Latter Rain Movement, as well as a protégé of William Branham, whom he calls "The Greatest Prophet Ever." But, he became disillusioned by the greed and pride he saw in the ministry, so he retired into semi-seclusion, living a life marked by scripture reading and prayer. He believed that God showed him to wait this way until the rise of the "New Breed" of men and women leaders who would be known by their "simplicity, purity, and remarkable manifestations of power." It was in a 1987 meeting with the leaders of the Kansas City Fellowship, that Cain decided that he had met his "New Breed!" Bob Jones bore witness to Cain, calling him the "Terror of the Lord or The Jealousy of God." This strong impression may have come about because of some of Cain's predictions, such as this one recorded in Al Dager's *Media Spotlight* article,

> "Jack Deere, a Vineyard Pastor, stated that in 1989 Cain told him an earthquake would occur on the same day Cain arrived for the first time to meet John Wimber at the Vineyard Church in Anaheim, California. Another would occur on the day he left Anaheim. According to Deere, Cain said the earthquake would be a confirmation that the Lord had a strategic purpose for the Vineyard Movement. A relatively minor earthquake common to Southern California shook Pasadena on the day Cain arrived. Cain claims that on the day after he left Anaheim, the Soviet-Armenian Earthquake occurred. But the records show that it occurred while Cain was still in Anaheim."

Another attestation to Cain's validity, in many people's minds, were the power surges that occurred at auditoriums where he held his meetings, blowing fuses, setting off fire alarms and even short circuiting video cameras! In one case, a battery operated video camera was surged and short circuited! Bickle may well have been referring to this when, after the outbreak of the Toronto Blessing, he attempted to help those who were experiencing various manifestations by publishing a paper entitled, "*God's Manifest Presence, Understanding the Phenomenon that Accompany the Spirit's Ministry*" which catalogued such manifestations as,

> "[S]haking, jerking, loss of bodily strength, heavy breathing, eyes fluttering, lips trembling, oil on body, changes in skin color...drunkenness...visions, hearing audibly into the spirit realm...jumping, violent rolling, screaming, nausea as discernment of evil, smelling or tasting good or evil

presence...feeling heavy weight or lightness, trances... disruption into the natural realm, i.e. circuits blown."

Amazingly all of the above and more, were presented as having been "observed in contemporary experience."

Like Jones and the other Kansas City Prophets, Cain held forth the standard Manifested Sons of God message, the birthing of the "new breed" of elite overcomers who would walk in power and glory, hitherto unknown in church history. They would purge the Old Order, and bring in the New Order, led by apostles and prophets. They would become the Joel's Army,

"You know this army...is also in the New Testament. It's referred to as the Manchild, Rev 12:5...the overcomers, Rev 2 and 3, the 144,000 servants, Rev. 7:3, the Bride or the Lamb's wife...the White Horse, Rev 6:2, the first fruits... the precious fruits...the wise virgins...the Manifested Sons of God...and its really remarkable...that none of these names are expressions applied to the saints of God or at any other time in history...they belong to this present generation...God's offering to the believers of this generation a greater privilege than was ever offered to any people of any generation at any time from Adam all the way down to the Millennium."

(Paul Cain, taped message)

Cain, in the manner of Branham, Jones, Bill Hamon, Rick Joyner, and others constantly prophesies a redefinition of Christianity based on the ministry of new prophets and apostles, which he calls, "the prize of all the ages."

"I think the most wonderful thing God is doing for us in these last days is raising up and restoring completely apostolic leadership, apostolic authority...the hope of the church, the hope of the world, is the apostolic ministry...So here God is raising up a new standard, a new banner, if you will, that's going to radically change the expression, the understanding of Christianity in our generation...God has invited us to have a role in establishing this New Order of Christianity...God is offering to this generation something He has never offered to any other generation before. He's giving us an open invitation to participate in something that will lead to the prize of all the ages...It's greater than anything He's ever done from Adam clear down through the millennium."

(Vineyard Prophecy School 1989)

It's flattering to hear prophecies that set us up as the "greatest generation," so great that nothing God has done down through time until now, compares with it. This flattery has disarmed countless bored believers who are seeking meaning for their lives.

By the early '90's, the Kansas City Prophets had begun to lose their luster, as their many false prophecies, wrong predictions, and the fallout in the lives of many who had been influenced by their "words," began to filter out. The Network of Christian Ministries was in the process of actually setting up a meeting to hold the Kansas City Prophets accountable on the basis of a paper written by a prominent Kansas City pastor documenting their errant teachings and practices. Before this happened, in the interest of making peace, John Wimber stepped forward and offered to bring the prophets under his "covering." This is the same Wimber who had completely been enamored of them a short time earlier! The Kansas City Fellowship became the Metro Vineyard of Kansas City, Paul Cain still ministers, worldwide. Bob Jones was exposed shortly thereafter for immorality and was asked to step down, though at this time he has been rehabilitated, and is currently recognized as a prophet. John Paul Jackson still ministers, and Mike Bickle is recognized as an authority on the "prophetic" and has written a book, *Growing in the Prophetic*, in which he still considers Bob Jones as a prophet of God! In a "Ministries" article, October, 1990, Bickle vehemently disagreed with the Kansas City pastor's charge that Jones was not a true prophet, but has acknowledged that Jones should not have been given a pulpit ministry. "I believe the Lord gave Bob Jones a backstage ministry, but I promoted him on the front stage," Bickle admitted. A recent prophecy of Jones' was that the Broncos won the Super Bowl last year as a sign, because their quarterback was named Elway,

"For my purpose is to get you to listen that I might show you El's Way...for you see in every thunderstorm, in every lightening strike, in every earthquake, in every volcano, I [God] have my way, for I AM ELWAY."

*(March 8, 1998. **Crossroads**. Hamilton, Ontario).*

Note

I. Bob Jones is not the Fundamentalist minister and Bible College founder, nor is he his son. As I explained in my other book, Weighed and Found Wanting, Bob Jones is an alleged prophet, prominent among the so-called "Kansas City Prophets."

Chapter Five

Rick Joyner—taking the Baton

"What is about to come upon the earth is not just a revival or another awakening, it is a veritable revolution. This vision was given in order to begin awakening those who are destined to radically change the course and even the very definition of Christianity."

(*The Harvest*. Rick Joyner)

"Homosexuality is having relations with your own sex. 'Spiritual Homosexuality' is also the desire to have relations only with your own kind. The Lord spelled this 'homo-sect-uality.' This is not meant to just be a funny play on words--it is a deadly serious condition in the church. Sectarianism is self-centeredness, self seeking, and self preservation that is the result of self-worship...Many of the world's great artists are homosexual. This lifestyle is so prevalent in the artistic community because, to a large degree, art as a true form of worship has been rejected by the church."

*(Joyner. **The Harvest**. Pages 74-75)*

The exposure of some of the false prophecies and errant practices of the Kansas City Prophets, and the subsequent disciplines imposed upon them by John Wimber, didn't chill the prophetic movement in any sense of the word. It only opened the door for the development of more prophetic ministries. It also served to further condition people to accept the idea of "prophets in training," not 100% accurate as Moses insisted, but evolutionary prophets, getting more accurate as they "practice" on people.

In 1989, at the height of the Kansas City prophets phenomenon, *The Harvest*, a 224 page prophecy by Rick Joyner burst upon the scene, to great acclaim, billing itself as "The prophetic word of the nineties." Since then,

Joyner's prophecies have received wide acceptance among the participants of the current renewal movement, including the Toronto Blessing people and the Pensacola Revival. *The Harvest* is a late 1980's prophecy foretelling the great move of the Spirit to come, and the things which must precede it, such as the complete dismantling of the "Old Order," (presumably meaning the old ecclesiastical order) to make room for the new. Joyner prophesies many warnings to leaders that,

"If the leaders resist this move, the Lord will continue to move through the congregations. These groups will begin to relate to other members of the Body of Christ and their bonds will grow stronger, regardless of the opposition from resistant pastors...the pastors and leaders who continue to resist this tide of unity will be removed from their place...Some that were greatly used of God in the past have become too rigid in doctrinal emphasis...to participate in this revival...Those who are linked together by doctrine or gathered around personalities will be quickly torn away...Some leaders will actually disband their organizations as they realize they are no longer relevant to what God is doing...A great company of prophets, teachers, pastors, and apostles will be raised up...This harvest will be so great that no one will be able to look back at the early church as a standard, all will be saying that the Lord saved the best for last."

I have selected these excerpts because many familiar themes are contained in it. Such as: the irrelevancy of many current ministries and their subsequent dismantling, the condemnation of those who have become "doctrinally rigid," contrasted to the coming "great company" of five-fold ministries (who by contrast, must not be doctrinally rigid), the New Order/Old Order theme, and the exaltation of this new breed coming, which is above all of the church down through time, "The best for last!" And of course, no prophetic utterance is complete without the warning to those who would resist. The "word" goes as far as prophesying insanity on them.

"Some pastors...who continue to resist this tide of unity will be removed from their place. Some will be so hardened they will become opposers and resist God to the end...This is the year when the Lord starts to bring down the spirit of Jezebel. He will begin by calling her to repentance. Those who have been vessels for this Spirit and who do not repent will be displayed as so insane that even the most immature Christians will discern their sickness."

Does this sound like the Lord of the church? Think! What is it that they are doing that could possibly bring this kind of judgement on them? We are not talking about Christ resisting communists here, nor satanists. This is a "prophecy" aimed at the shepherds of the Lord's flock! What did they do to bring insanity on themselves, so obvious that everyone can see it? Did they renounce their vows? Reject Jesus? Blaspheme from the pulpit? This threat is leveled at people who have given their life to serve Jesus' flock, often for no glory (and no gold) and their only sin was to reject this so called Revival! This intimidation is effective enough, for these are tough times to be in the pastorate, especially if you happen to be shepherding a "little flock." The bluster of these supposed men of God who appear to be successful (by this world's standards), their arrogance, and "great swelling words" can be intimidating, in this day of outward appearances. And more than one pastor, toiling in obscurity, losing people who want to be "where the action is" have been swept into the revival against their better judgement. Therefore, these unchristlike threats will be answerable before the Throne of God, the true shepherd!

And yet, out of the abundance of the heart, the mouth doth speak (and prophesy). That is why so much of the prophecy (when it is not attempting to bully people with threats) is about how great the modern apostles and prophets are. As The Harvest brings out,

"It was said of the Apostle Paul that he was turning the world upside down...it will be said of the apostles soon to be anointed that they have turned the world right side up. Nations will tremble at the mention of their name."

Did Peter and Paul want nations to tremble at the mention of their name? Did they go about prophesying of their exploits? Only in this self absorbed generation would such a prophesy even remotely be considered a word from God.

The theme of the rejection of the leadership of the "old order" of the church consistently recurs in this ministry, as in this prophecy, from a 1990 Harvest Conference,

> "We are all members of one another and we must start acting like the church as a body...we have come to a time of spiritual revolution...Benjamin Franklin said 'We've gotta join or die,' is becoming increasingly applicable to the church, those who refuse to tear down the walls, I tell you the people are going to do it...And just as those of the former order who did not recognize that a new order had come upon the church--that there is a new order today...Some of the most penetrating scenes that I saw in the news last year were the communist leaders who...had been some of the most powerful people in this world, were on their knees begging the people to listen to them and the people were saying, 'Away with you we will never listen to you again.' A New Order has come, I tell you, you are going to see the same things taking place in the church."

What a vision! Who is this tyrannical enemy that is so cursed that he will either be displayed as insane, or the people will publically reject him, as they did cruel communist dictators like Ceaucescu? The answer? Pastors. Pentecostal, evangelical, often little appreciated, usually without flair, in danger often of being abandoned by fickle entertainment saturated people, who are ever learning and never coming to the knowledge of the truth. And what is the crime that deserves such reproach as insanity or open and public rejection? Not going along with the "New Order."

Joyner is very much active in the prophetic ministry to this day. His latest offering is *The Final Quest*, published by Whitaker House. The 158 page prophecy contains what Joyner refers to as "some strategic revelations." The visions it contains are said to "illuminate some doctrines." His first vision is entitled "The Hordes of Hell are Marching." It describes a cosmic battle, the Army of God versus the Hordes of Hell. The demonic army, in full battle array, rides not on horses, but on the backs of "well dressed, respectable...refined and educated" Christians!! The disgusting vision describes the demons as vomiting, defecating, and urinating on the Christians who mistook the above for the "Truth of God" and for the "Anointing of the Holy Spirit!" The battle that will soon come, Joyner says, will be known by many as "The Great Christian Civil War." This American Civil War motif has also been prophesied by James Ryle, Bob Jones, Wes and Stacy Campbell, and other prophets. In the surreal world of the prophets, symbolism takes on a life of its own. The Blues in the army have been interpreted as those who are operating on revelation knowledge, blue being symbolic of heaven. The Grays, are still operating out of their heads (gray matter, the brain, get it?) The Gray Army (of Christians) are seeking to hold the church in "spiritual slavery."

Getting back to Joyner's *The Final Quest* vision of the Hordes of Hell riding on the backs of Christians who think that the demonic vomit and defecation and urine is the "Truth of God." A figure Joyner knows as the Angel Wisdom, guides Joyner through his vision, which is full of interesting details, such as talking eagles, ascending a multilevel mountain, and arrows which represent Bible truths. As Joyner ponders the meaning of his vision, he wrote these words,

> "A great Civil War now looms before the church...the Lord is now preparing a leadership that will be willing to fight a Civil War in order to set men free. The main issue will be slavery versus freedom...The church will not be destroyed, but the institutions and doctrines that have kept men in spiritual slavery will be. Even after this, perfect justice in the church will not be attained overnight. There will be struggles for women's rights and to set the church free from other forms of racism and exploitation."
>
> *(The Final Quest. Page 37)*

It would be helpful to know what Joyner and other "prophets" are specifically referring to when they accuse a good number of Christians of "spiritual slavery." And just what doctrines are these prophets crying out against? Add racism, exploitation, and oppression of women to the list of sins Joyner believes the "Old Order" is responsible. But posturing themselves as the Union Army, the new prophets aspire to be saviors, attaining "perfect justice," "women's rights," and racial equality! The only reason I think we should talk about these vain imaginations is because thousands of Christians have taken *The Final Quest* seriously!

The remainder of *The Final Quest* reads like an apocryphal book. Much of it is dialogue with the Angel Wisdom who also came to him in the form of a talking eagle. Joyner also is allowed to interview the apostle Paul, one of the reformers, and numerous departed saints. Through the talking eagle, Joyner is given such nuggets as this,

> "Even though you have climbed to the top of the mountain, and have received from every truth along the way, and even though you have stood in the garden of God, tasted of His unconditional love, and have seen His Son many times now, you still understand only a part of the whole counsel of God and that only superficially."

The angel Wisdom teaches Joyner and the church,

> " 'The Lord dwells within. You have taught this many times but now must live it for you have eaten of the tree of Life.' The Angel then began to lead me back to the gate (out of Paradise). I protested that I didn't want to leave. Looking surprised, the Angel took me by the shoulders and looked me in the eyes, that is when I recognized him as the Angel Wisdom. 'You never have to leave this garden, this garden is in your heart because the Creator Himself is within you.' "

Joyner forces thinking Christians into a decision, for he is not saying, "I think it is like this," (allegorically) nor is he offering a controversial exegesis of scripture, that would be debatable. He claims to have interacted with angels, had visions, talked to spiritual eagles who talked back to him and, like the mystics of old, climbed "the Holy Mountain." Either he is lying or telling the truth about his experiences. There is no reason to believe that he is lying, therefore we can assume that he had these experiences. The question is, did Joyner actually speak to an angel of God? Did he receive from the Lord the vision of the "Hordes of Hell," defecating and vomiting on Christians? Because this man has been set forth as a prophet of God, loyalty to God demands that we take a critical look at his ministry.

Chapter Six

Other Prophets

"We stand at the most crucial crossroads in the history of our nation! We must hear the Word of the Lord that will prepare our way into the next century! The future generations depend on this word! The prophetic streams across this nation are uniting to sound a clear trumpet for the future! This uniting of the streams will form the bedrock for revelation for the River of Revival! Prophets help to prepare the way for the Apostles to establish the Lord's Church."
(Advertisement for C.P. Wagner's "School of Prophets" Conference).

One of the most prominent and influential of the new prophets is Bill Hamon. As the founder of Christian International Ministries, he has been in the prophetic ministry for forty years, and has dedicated much of his ministry to the restoration of the office of the prophet. Hamon is considered by many to be the father of the prophetic movement, and he dedicated his book, *Prophets and Personal Prophecy* to "the great company of prophets God is raising up in these last days." He has been holding prophetic conferences and a school of the prophets for almost twenty years and is considered by many to be one of the leading prophetic voices of our day. His book sets forth the theology of the prophetic movement,

"The prophets are being brought forth to fulfill their part in preparing the Bride-Church for her day of presentation to her heavenly Bridegroom, Christ Jesus. Jesus is rejoicing with great joy over the part the prophets are playing in preparing his Bride. When the prophets have finished their ministry, He will be released to descend from heaven with a shout and be fully

and eternally united with his Bride. Twentieth century prophets are very precious to Christ, for they are perfecting the Bride He died to purchase, the church."
(Prophets and Personal Prophecy. Bill Hamon. Page 25).

As you can see, this is nothing more than the mancentered Manifested Sons of God theology, which has Jesus waiting to be "released" by us, the last days cutting edged, victorious church! In this case, He awaits the new prophets to perfect His Bride. Hamon states in the same chapter that "Jesus is thrilled at the thought that His prophets will soon be fully recognized and accepted by His Church."

On the contrary, the only apostles and prophets that it is essential that the church recognize are the ones who have given us the New Testament. It is the faith, "Once and for all given to the saints" that the church has been founded on, not "twentieth century prophets and apostles." One would get the idea that Jesus is being held back from returning because the church has failed to receive prophets like Rick Joyner, Bob Jones, and Bill Hamon!

The Latter Rain/Manifested Sons of God Theology is flawed in that it often confuses the person of Christ with the Body of Christ, the church. To the church are

often assigned the prerogatives and responsibilities that are reserved for Christ alone! It is Christ Jesus who Himself will subdue all of God's enemies, including Death itself, not the church. The hope of the ages is the Parousia, the actual physical return of Christ Jesus, not the "Great Last Days Revival," or the "Restoration of the new apostles and prophets." The purposes of God are wrapped up in Jesus Christ, and it is in Him that has come and remains in the flesh. It has never been about man, "we must decrease and He must increase" according to the "greatest prophet born of a woman," John the Baptist.

The new prophets dream of a day of dazzling worldly influence, as can be seen in the following "word,"

"The President of the United States and heads of nations will begin to seek out the Christian prophets and prophetic ministers to find out what is really taking place and to know what to do. World conditions will come to the place that human hearts will be failing them for fear. The manipulators that control the economy, stock market, and world banking systems will lose their control. God will cut their puppet strings and take things out of their hands. Only those who know how to hear and speak the true mind of Christ and the Word of God will have the answers. The Joseph and Daniel Prophetic company will arise with the supernatural answers for the needs of the Egyptian Pharaohs, and Babylonian emperors of this world. The prophetic church will finally demonstrate fully that Jesus Christ really is the answer for the world-not only to save them from their sins, but to bring peace on earth and goodwill toward all people."

(Prophets and the Prophetic Movement. Bill Hamon)

This desire for the church to have such worldly influence is nothing new. This has been the ambition of the Roman Catholic Church for centuries. That such prophecies would be unquestioningly accepted by Pentecostals and Evangelicals is amazing. This is a sign to us to show just how far we have been conditioned by MSOG concepts. Whatever happened to "You will be hated by all nations for my name sake?" "No we won't, Lord! We are so anointed these days, heads of nations seek out our prophets and apostles! Isn't that great?" This is vastly more appealing than, "Will the Son of Man find faith when he comes to the earth?"

I can't emphasize enough the man-centered nature of both the Latter Rain/MSOG doctrine and the prophetic movement that came out of it. Supposedly by accepting these new prophets and their "words," WE, the church, can usher in the presence of the Lord, supposedly, for it is only after our triumph over the enemies of Christ that He will be "released" to return.

"When the church has put under it's feet all the enemies of Christ that he has ordained for them to subdue, then Christ can be released from heaven to return as the Manifested Head of His Physically Resurrected and Translated Church."

*(Bill Hamon. **The Eternal Church.** Page 333).*

The Toronto Blessing and the Pensacola Revival that came out of it, have both been heavily influenced by prophetic ministries. Both of them claim to have been the result of prophecies given by David Yonggi Cho, the world famous pastor of the world's largest Christian congregation, which is in South Korea. They are also both seen by many as being the direct fulfillment of many of Paul Cain's and Bob Jones' prophecies, as is Promise Keepers. New prophets are frequently given platforms in these and similar meetings.

The Toronto Airport Vineyard actually had its own "in house" prophet, long before the Toronto Blessing hit. His name is Marc Dupont, and he had prophesied in 1992 that "Like Jerusalem, Toronto will be center from which many are sent out to the nations," and that leaders would come from around the world to receive from the anointing there. He prophesied again in 1993 that he "sensed from the Lord an extreme danger for leaders who continue to resist the Holy Spirit," concerning the coming revival in Toronto. Interestingly, all of this occurred before there was any "Toronto Blessing."

Dupont's prophetic message calls for revival on the grounds that the church has become dull, uninspiring, and worse yet "religious." Another critique that he has frequently offered is that the church is more interested in the Bible than they are in the person of Jesus.

> "The churches are basically houses of Bible study, and not of prayer."
>
> ("Holy Ghost Train," cassette message).

To Dupont, church leaders are all too often guilty of resistance to the Holy Ghost, but the Holy Ghost will not be deterred,

> "The Holy Spirit has been rude enough to start ministry on His own without consulting the speakers." (Ibid).

Intellectualism in the church is also much criticized as a hindrance to the revival. In a taped message entitled, "The Father's Heart and the Prophetic" Dupont places the blame for the fall of man on intellectualism, and teaches that the barrenness of Michal, David's wife, Saul's daughter, was also a result of the same.

> "There is a barrenness because we have been clinging to ourselves, we've been trying to control the situation. It's as if with our continual focus on teaching, teaching, preaching...filling ourselves up."

When Dupont and others equate teaching and preaching with barrenness (in their own teachings) they set up an artificial tension between knowing Jesus and the knowledge of God (theology). As if those who seek the knowledge of God are dry and dead, while those who reject theology for unmediated experience are assumed to be "heart people" who truly know God. Dupont again,

> "We [Christians] love the truth about Jesus more than we love Jesus Himself."

I believe that the cumulative effect of this steady stream of now in teaching is cynicism and discontented unbelief, which breaks down any reasonable objections to the ministry of these New Breed Prophets. The last shreds of discernment are further torn down by constant charges like the following,

> "Christians have more confidence in Satan or the AntiChrist to deceive us than we have in the Holy Spirit to lead us and guide us into all truth."
>
> *("Lion of Judah," cassette message)*

What can one do? When you have already consented to the charge that the church is dead, religious, uptight, critical and even Pharisaical, and all of this from a man widely received as a prophet from God! Dupont and Joyner have been very effective in shaming God's people away from critical thinking, and through well turned phrases like,

> "[W]e can understand how it works in our heads...but God is not God the Father, God the Son and God the Holy Bible."
>
> (Dupont. Ibid)

For those who still hold out against the rising tide of mysticism there is an increasingly ominous tone to the many prophecies,

> "And so at the same time that churches that are responding to the Spirit are going to get more and more filled up with freedom and liberty and joy, and the peace and everything in the Kingdom, I believe that there's also going to come stricter and stricter judgement. I believe judgement this year is radically increasing, especially leaders that are going to stand in a Pharisaical stance and are going to attack what God is doing."
>
> *(Prophetic School. Marc Dupont. 1994).*

And what constitutes a "Pharisaical stance?" If anything, it seems not to be a description of those who oppose Jesus Christ and salvation by grace, as the real Pharisees. Rather it is their description of those who offer criticism of the mysticism that has exploded on the earth with the advent of the Toronto Blessing. These new prophets pronounce judgement, as if their concept of "what God is doing in the nineties" is on the same level as the coming of Jesus to save us from our sins. Pronounce judgement on those who reject Jesus, or pervert the gospel of salvation by grace, for the Bible itself tells us "How shall we escape if we neglect so great a salvation?" But to pronounce the same judgement on God fearing pastors and Christians, who actually preach the gospel and love Jesus, but whose only "fault" is their failure to recognize the Toronto Blessing or Rodney Howard Browne, as valid moves of God is reprehensible! But this is exactly what the new prophets are unafraid to do.

> "By the late nineties...Judgement is very much going to increase to the point where I believe that many leaders who are fighting what the Spirit of God is doing and saying, God is going to take them out of the ministry. I believe some of them, I know this isn't new, other people have said this, but I do believe it's true, that God is going to be taking some leaders home to heaven, rather than continue to allow them to mislead God's people."
> (Ibid).

If critical thinking, *à la* the Bereans, is a vice to these people, openness to a wide array of extreme manifestations is a virtue. When I tell you extreme, I am not kidding. The expression "Laughing Revival" doesn't do justice to the actual experiences of many. Perhaps a more apt term would be the Mystical Revival. Dupont again,

> "God is not a gentleman, God is God! God is not the great I WAS or I WILL BE, right now, the dirty now and now, not the sweet by and by. Quite often when God's Spirit comes it is a little more than crazy. How the Son of God comes on people! I've seen glasses fly across the room, I've seen marriage bands fly off fingers, I've seen boots and shoes fly off people, we've seen people destroy their clothes, almost being thrashed by the Holy Spirit."

Really? Does this sound like the Holy Spirit? The very Spirit of Truth who came to lead us into all truth? This is more reminiscent of the account in Acts 19 of the seven sons of Sceva. This is not to say that the Holy Spirit is a passive, orderly being. He is God himself, He is sovereign, and cannot be controlled. However, we do have a frame of reference with which to critically evaluate what are called manifestations of the Spirit.

The impartation concept, introduced in the Latter Rain Revival, is alive and well, and with quite a bit of intensity in Dupont's experience,

> "It's one of the more scary things I've ever seen as 300 people were receiving 'major prophetic impartations' and were being shaken like rag dolls."

I want to emphasize at this point that it is neither my intention nor my responsibility to judge the motives of prophets such as Dupont and Joyner, who both seem to be sincerely attempting to be obedient to the Lord. Sincerity is no safeguard against deception, however. There is definitely something spiritual and powerful working in these ministries. People who have been touched by them have been radicalized. Can you imagine how hard you would have to be shaken to thrash off your wedding ring? To destroy your clothes? But what Spirit is working here? 300 people being shaken like rag dolls? Why didn't Peter and Paul minister this?

There are other Toronto prophets like Stacy and Wes Campbell, who are pastors of a fellowship in British Columbia. Wes Campbell testifies of the sudden inundation of his church with the prophetic, well before the Toronto Blessing. I quote him in my book *Weighed and Found Wanting*, Putting the Toronto Blessing in Context, where he relates the channeling of the Holy Spirit through a man in the church! When the man would come into the influence of the "Spirit," they would be able to ask "God" questions, which would be answered through the man's utterances!! That this would be an accepted form of divine communion is an example of the level of discernment many have operated on. God doesn't channel, He is not "trying to say something," "God has spoken to us in His Son" once and for all! Stacy Campbell, his wife, is considered to be a prophetess in the movement and there are several widely distributed prophecies which feature her prophesying while she whips her head about violently, and uttering breathlessly. It sends an otherworldly chill down the spine to see it, bringing to mind the Delphic Oracle. She also, as Bob Jones, Rick Joyner, and James Ryle, has prophesied of a coming "Civil War" in the church.

James Ryle

The pastor of the Boulder Vineyard, and mentor to Bill McCartney of Promise Keepers, is also a prophet. His name is James Ryle. He is an important figure in our discussion of the modern day prophets because of his wide influence, which can be seen through Promise Keepers, as well as through his books on the subject of prophecy and dream interpretation, *Hippo in the Garden* and *A Dream Come True*. Perhaps one of his best known and most controversial prophecies was given in a message entitled "Sons of Thunder." Ryle prophesied that the Beatles (as in John, Paul, George, and Ringo) were at one time anointed by the Holy Spirit to bring in worldwide revival through music.

"[Quotes Psalm 68:18]...The Lord spoke to me and said, 'What you saw in the Beatles--the gifting and the sound they had-was from Me. It did not belong to them, it belonged to Me. And it was My purpose to bring forth through music a worldwide revival that would usher in the move of my Spirit in bringing in men and women to Christ... And I want to tell you those four lads, they aborted something. They took what did not belong to them and used it in a way that was not intended by God to be used. It did bring in a revival of music-but it brought it on the other side of the fence-if you know what I am saying.' And the Lord spoke to me and He said, 'In 1970 I lifted the anointing off of them. And it has been held in my hand ever since...that anointing belongs to the church.'"

Ryle's message goes on to say that he saw a vision of a Sergeant Pepper's Lonely Hearts Club Band record jacket,
"Floating down and he knew that represented the anointing, the mantle, the covering that was coming to the 'Sons of Thunder.' And not long ago, the Lord said, 'I'm giving you permission to pass the jacket out.' "
(James Ryle, "Sons of Thunder." Harvest Conference, Denver Colorado, November, 1990).

Need we say any more of this widely acclaimed prophet? John Wimber prophesied that Ryle would be a seer to the Body of Christ, and in that same year, Ryle had a dream of a hippo standing in a garden, which was interpreted to mean that a new prophetic movement would be sweeping the church and impacting the whole world. (*Charisma*, Aug.1993, "James Ryle: From Prisoner to Preacher").

There are many others who are prominent in this prophetic movement, these are a mere sampling. Hundreds and even thousands have been touched and influenced by William Branham, The Kansas City Prophets, Rick Joyner, Paul Cain, James Ryle, Morris Cerullo, Earl Paulk, Bill Hamon, and dozens of others who are vigorously promoting the movement of new prophets and apostles. How should the church respond to them? Are there reliable, objective tests to submit them to? What do they say about these tests? What is a responsible theology of the prophetic? These are some of the questions we will now consider.

Chapter Seven

Judging Prophetic Ministry

"Despise not prophesyings. Prove all things; hold fast to that which is good."

l *Thessalonians* 5:20-21

"I think that the church...is reacting in fear today...people are saying, 'Oh be careful, be careful!...be careful what you read, be careful who lays hands on you'...that's all fine, but if you play it safe with this thing, the Holy Spirit, you know what? You're never going to get anywhere...See we need to have more faith in God's ability to bless then Satan's ability to deceive."

(John Arnott, Toronto Airport Vineyard, Dec. 1994)

The two quotes above illustrate for us the contrasting views of an approach to New Testament prophecy and prophetic ministry. The New Testament does not support the cessationist view, for we are plainly commanded not to despise prophetic utterance. But, on the other hand, neither does the New Testament support current Charismatic attitudes for we are also emphatically commanded to "Prove [judge] all things." The gifts of the Spirit are not the problem, it is the abuse and manipulation of people in the name of the gifts, that we are currently struggling with. Fear and reaction are not current problems either, for to be discerning, and even cautious, is a matter of loyalty to God. Those who would manipulate God's people into passive acceptance of unscriptural practices, have become adept at labeling the discerning believers as being "religious" or "in reaction," and as some kind of unbelievers. The truth is, to believe Jesus is to take seriously

51

His admonition that "there shall be false Christs..and if it were possible, they should deceive the very elect." (Matthew 24:24). Note, that he said false "Christs" not false "Jesus.' " Why is this significant? The current proclamation is that many are now operating under a "New Anointing," never before experienced in the church, but now revealed for the "Last Days cutting edged church." Not a "New Jesus," but a "New Anointing." The word Christ, is a transliteration of the Greek word which means "Anointed One." A "false Christ" is nothing more or less than a falsely anointed one.

It is at least suspect for so called spokesmen for God to be shaming people out of critically evaluating the new spiritual experiences that have been springing forth lately. Especially when such strong claims have been made of them by their proponents. Anything so significant that to resist it is to endanger one's life, ministry and in some cases their very salvation, should at least call for some biblical scrutiny. These are the claims being made by the leaders in "the River," the Toronto Blessing, the prophetic movement, and so forth. The severest and most fervent railings have been hurled at those who would dare raise questions, and at least ask of God's people that they think somewhat critically. What a contrast to the Bible, which declares of the Bereans that they were "noble" because they wouldn't even blindly accept the Apostle Paul until they had checked him out through their Bibles. We are to judge all things, and cling tightly to anything that is good and abhor that which is evil! And he stated this in the context of New Testament prophecy!

There are a few things I would like to bring out at the outset, hopefully to give some perspective to all of this. First, there is a difference between the gift of prophecy and the prophetic office. Acts 21 brings the contrast out for us, in speaking of the evangelist Philip it states,

"And the same man had four daughters, virgins, which did prophesy." (Acts 21:9)

But in the next verse we learn that,

"And as we tarried there many days, there came down from Judea a certain Prophet, named Agabus." (Acts 21:10)

52

There is a difference between someone who stands in a Pentecostal worship service and believes they have received an utterance, "Unto edification, exhortation and comfort" (I Corinthians 14:3), and someone who assumes the position of an Agabus, an Elijah, Isaiah or a Jeremiah. In the gift of prophecy, an utterance may or may not have been given unto them to encourage the Body, or it may have been them thinking they had a Word, when it really wasn't God. This can be corrected, and First Corinthians brings this out. God gives people utterances, encouragements, thoughts, impressions etc.

However, this being used to prophesy, unto edification, exhortation and comfort, is a far cry from assuming the role of a prophet of the Living God! If I fail to receive a prophecy in a church service, I have cheated myself out of perhaps some much needed encouragement. But, if I disregard a prophet that the Lord sent unto me, that is a serious matter! Therefore, it is a far more serious thing to proclaim yourself to be a prophet, then it is to be used to give an encouraging utterance in a church. When Kenneth Hagin gave his message, "How To Write Your Own Ticket With God," he didn't say that he found this teaching in scripture. If he had, we would be in a position to possibly debate it or accept it or even think, "He's a good man, but I don't agree with his interpretation of scripture." We don't have that option, for Hagin tells us, Jesus himself appeared to him and taught him this! It's not a matter of interpretation now. Hagin, who bills himself as a Prophet of God, is presenting this as direct revelation from Jesus Christ Himself! This forces earnest and Godfearing believers to have to decide, "If I believe that Jesus told him this am bound to have to live by it," but if Jesus didn't tell him this, he is either lying, in the name of the Lord, or he really did have a spiritual experience, but was wrong about it's source." Now if that is true, what spirit appeared to Hagin teaching him (and us) things about God? And claiming to be Jesus? Can you see the dilemma here? We don't have the luxury here to grant that we don't accept the particular interpretation, but Hagin is still a man of God. When people come forth with open dreams, visions, revelations, interactions with angels, and unmediated experiences in places like the throne room of God, whether we accept the responsibility or not, we are all forced into severe decisions.

53

Either they are "on" or "off." Of God or of the devil. There can be no middle ground!

This goes for predictions also. When New Testament prophets made predictions, they always came to pass. For example, Agabus predicted a "dearth throughout all the world, which came to pass in the days of Claudius Caesar" (Acts 11:28). He was also used of God to warn Paul of the plots of the Jews to bind him in Acts 20. This also came to pass. Predictions in the name of the Lord are very serious business, as Deuteronomy 18 points out, and if there was some kind of new leniency toward inaccurate predictions in the New Testament, why are there no inaccurate predictions recorded there?

Do I believe there are prophets living today? Absolutely! The ascension gift ministries of Ephesians 4:11 are needed now more than ever. But we must take another look at the function of prophets in the Bible, and get away from the modern model of a prophet. The prophets of the Bible: Isaiah, Jeremiah, Daniel, John the Baptist, Agabus, and the prophets mentioned in Acts 13, were not those who went around having conferences, giving everyone personal "words," inner healings, zapping people, cursing their detractors, etc. Prophets were and are preachers and teachers raised up for the purpose of calling God's people back unto Him when they have fallen away. In the process of those teachings and preachings, predictions were made that attested to the validity of the messengers, and their message. Sure there are prophets these days, and God validates their ministry as He sees fit. But the signs and wonders are not ends in themselves. The most important part is the message.

Another important distinction is the fact that Ephesians 2:20 has been fulfilled once and for all. It states,

"And [ye] are built upon the foundation of the apostles and prophets, Jesus Christ Himself being the chief cornerstone." (Ephesians 2:20)

Why is this an important distinction? Because this verse is currently being interpreted by many to mean that your very spiritual foundation is dependant upon these new prophets, and to fail to submit to this ministry is to somehow leave you without a foundation. The apostles and prophets that the whole church is founded upon are the prophets of the Old Testament and the Apostles of the New. These are your foundation. Everything should be "plumbed" according to the apostles and anything which contradicts their teaching is not of God.

"WE [the apostles] are of God, he that knoweth God heareth us, he that is not of God heareth not us, Hereby we know the Spirit of Truth and the Spirit of Error." (1 John 4:6)

The God of the Bible is not currently "Trying to say something to the church." He has spoken unto us through His Son. He has given us a "more sure word of prophecy, which you would do well to take heed." That Word is final and authoritative. Any modern prophet is going to be raised up to call people back to that sure Word even as Isaiah and Jeremiah were used to summon the children of Israel back to Moses, and to faithfulness to the God of Israel. Their messages were straight out of the Torah. They preached sermons, expounded on the broken Law of God, the applications of His Holy penalties, the beauty of His attributes, and the main theme, Christ himself! In the process of all of this they did indeed make predictions, which always related to the Messiah, and to God's purposes for Israel and the nations.

This linkage of prophets with teachers and preachers carries right over into the New Testament. "There were false prophets among them even as there shall be false teachers among you." (2 Peter 2:1). This is extremely important to us, for the tests that Moses gave us for true or false prophets in Deuteronomy also carry over and are assumed in the New Testament. When the Apostles said "test all things" or "try the Spirit" they were assuming that there was a basic familiarity with the tests, for there is no elaborate description of them. Thankfully, though the tests carry over, the penalty does not, for the church is not a theocratic national entity as Israel was. We don't stone false prophets though the sin is no less serious! Certainly, false prophecy brings spiritual death and disillusionment wherever it is allowed unchecked.

There are two tests for prophets in Deuteronomy, one in chapter 13, and the other in chapter 18. Chapter 18 is the more simple and straightforward of the two,

"When a prophet speaketh in the name of the Lord, if the thing follow not, nor come to pass, that is the thing that the Lord has not spoken, but the prophet has spoken presumptuously: thou shall not be afraid of him." (Deut 18:22).

As I said, this is very simple. God's prophets are 100% accurate in their pronouncements. God wants his flock to be able to tell right away who is and isn't of God! He is not giving you an ambiguous, subjective test here, such as "Does he seem to Love Jesus?" which can be easily faked. For a literal example of this, in 1994, Paul and Jan Crouch hosted a prophet named John Hinckle on their show who predicted that on June 9th of that year, "All evil would be ripped off of the earth." Obviously, by June 10, it should have been obvious to all that was a false prophecy. It should have been, of course, but these days the conditioning has been so consistent that many were hard pressed to know what to do about it! This man seemed so loving and sincere (as if false prophets have fangs and wear a long black cape).

So many have already been disillusioned, and some have even lost their faith because of this toleration of false prophets! The prophets themselves, in many cases, after having dabbled at being a "seer," intoxicated by the power that many attribute to them, have gone on to shipwreck their faith. Adding insult to injury the New Breed of prophets have devised ingenious ways of theologizing around the tests that the Lord instituted for His flock's safety, and also they have turned the responsibility for their failed prophecies back on to the recipients of them. "It didn't come to pass, because you lacked faith."

The second test for true and false prophets is more subtle. Suppose you have a prophet whose predictions do come to pass? His words to people seem accurate, he even seems to have the power to heal, people are getting "results" and seem to be being helped. Can we now automatically assume that all is well? Is God indeed blessing and endorsing this ministry? Not necessarily. Deuteronomy 13:13 speaks to this issue,

"If there arises among you a prophet or a dreamer of dreams, and giveth you a sign or a wonder, and the sign or the wonder comes to pass, whereof he spake unto thee saying, 'Let us go after other gods, which thou hast not known, and let us serve them,' thou shalt not hearken unto the words of that prophet, or dreamer of dreams, for the Lord your God would prove you, to know whether you love the Lord your God with all your heart and all your soul." (Deuteronomy 13:13)

Of course it should be obvious that very few false prophets would come into a Christian church and announce, "Let us go after other gods and serve them!" In fact, I am convinced that most false prophets have no idea, either that they are leading people after false gods, or that they are indeed false prophets! Deuteronomy 13 calls our attention to a principle, that when seeking to determine the validity of a ministry, in this case prophets, don't focus on the "signs and wonders" nor the "results," to the exclusion of focusing on the message, the teaching! Remember that signs, wonders, predictions, and other results of any ministry, only attest to the message that ministry brings. They are not ends in themselves. These days the focus is very much upon the spectacular, the miracles or promise of them. Deuteronomy ought to alert us to the fact that in some instances, God will actually allow false prophets to arise and seem to "have the goods," that He might test His people, to see if they "Love the Lord their God with all of their heart." Love God? Of course we love God! We have never had such zeal and Love, the church has never been so "on fire." There has never been such an abundance of worship in all of church history! But this is loving God on our terms, and not God's. How do you know you truly love God? To God, love is translated as loyalty, and loyalty to His Word.

Alas, as in the days of William Branham, we are currently minimizing the teachings of the new prophets and maximizing their alleged signs and wonders. We are so generous though, for when some prophet does make an inaccurate prediction, or brings forth some outrageously unorthodox teaching, we grant that "He may get a little off at times, but his heart is in the right place, and God seems to be endorsing him, he has the power." We were given a number of clear cut chances to pass the Deuteronomy 13 test, as Pentecostals and Charismatics, but we seem to continuously flunk them.

We have mentioned William Branham as an example of a clear cut Deuteronomy 13 test. There were many Pentecostal leaders who sought to convince Branham to play down his unorthodox teachings, so that he could continue to gain acceptance in Pentecostal churches. As long as he stayed with his sign gift ministry, it didn't matter what he personally believed, "people are getting results." For some time Branham actually did limit his extreme revelations to his own Jeffersonville, Indiana congregation. He downplayed His "Serpent's Seed" revelation and his abhorrence of the doctrine of the Trinity, so that he would be accepted in "Trinitarian" churches. Today, unfortunately, the lesson of William Branham is still misunderstood, in too many cases. The popular opinion is that Branham didn't have a teaching ministry, so he should have avoided teaching. He missed his call, he was a prophet, and a healer, not a teacher. To them the lesson is, "Don't stray out of your calling." Wrong!!! The real message should be shouted from the housetops, "Prophets are teachers and preachers, they always have a message. Don't judge them by their 'results,' but by their message! Just because they can make accurate predictions or tell you something about your life, or even heal you, doesn't mean they are sent by God!" Mormons have signs and wonders. Marriages have come together, people have quit smoking, and there have been people who became upright citizens as a result of Mormonism! But it is of the Spirit of Antichrist! The fruit of a prophet, or a movement or a revival can be evaluated by the consistent teaching. (Matthew 12:33-35).

Of course Branham had never gotten up and said, "Let us go after other gods," as far as I can tell he was a profoundly sincere and humble man. But again, so was Edgar Cayce. However, the God of Branham's Angel, is not the God of the Bible. The God who inspired the Serpent's Seed teaching, with it's hatred of women and its racial undertones is certainly not the God of the Bible. The Spirit who told Branham that the Zodiac, the Great Pyramid, and the scriptures were all valid words from God, is definitely not the Holy Spirit. Nor is the god of Rodney Howard Browne's "Holy Ghost Bartender" ministry, or the god of Rick Joyner's talking Eagle, Bob Jones' Civil War, and his "Dominus" vision. The spirit who taught James Ryle that the Beatles were anointed by the Holy Spirit until 1970

(The year they broke up), is not the God of Daniel and Isaiah. The Jesus who told Kenneth Hagin how he could "write his own ticket with God" is certainly not Jesus the Messiah. The God of the Bible is not localizing Himself in cities like Pensacola or Toronto, so that little churches all over the world can charter buses there to get "it" (the anointing). But if we were to go by external "results," all of these are validated by signs and wonders, changed lives, healings and habits being broken. It is not our place to judge their motives either positively or negatively, but it is our responsibility to judge the message.

John, in I John chapter 4, confirms this test, when he puts forth a doctrinal standard for prophets, "Any Spirit that confesses not that Jesus Christ has come [and remains] in the flesh is not of God but is of the Antichrist." This is the New Testament version of Deuteronomy 13, warning us that the Antichrist can be known by a consistent teaching which spiritualizes the person of Jesus. The word "confesseth" does not refer to an ability or inability to say "Jesus has come and remains in the flesh," but rather it refers to the consistent teaching of the ministry. For example, a Jehovah's Witness, when pressed, can easily say the confession of the incarnation, but when the overall doctrine is evaluated, There is a consistent denial of the incarnation, that God come unto us in the flesh, in the person of Jesus Christ.

In summary, the tests for prophets are found in Deuteronomy 13, and 18. Prophets are to be regarded not as wonder workers, giving personal words, blowing people away with signs and wonders, but always as messengers. Therefore, the message is what justifies or condemns the prophetic ministry, not the results in people's lives. That message is always either humanistic, demonic, or a Word from the God of scripture. God will test His people, from time to time, on their love. Love on His terms means loyalty to His truth.

Chapter Eight

Prophetic Evasion

"The prophet who misses it occasionally in his prophecies may be ignorant, immature, or presumptuous, or he may be ministering with too much zeal and too little wisdom and anointing. But this does not prove him a false prophet..it is certainly possible for a true prophet to be inaccurate."
*(Bill Hamon. **Prophets and Personal Prophecy**).*

"When it comes to something such as personal prophecy, we believe that extremism is more deadly than when dealing with less volatile issues. That is because there is an element of control involved when one individual is able to speak for God to a group of individuals...We believe there are some who purport to prophesy that actually get their unusual ability to know the future, not from the Holy Spirit, but from the Spirit of Divination. And there are some Charismatics who are so eager to know God's will or get a Word from God or to be singled out in a service where this special gift may be manifest that they are susceptible to spirits that are not from God."
*(Stephan Strang. Charisma Magazine. **"A Caution On Personal Prophecy."** Sept. 1989).*

One consistent characteristic of the new prophets is their insistence that the New Testament prophets do not have to be subjected to the Deuteronomy tests. They are incredibly resourceful in the many ways that they rationalize this position. But, the end result is that there is no objective standard by which to measure them, for those who accept their reasoning. I have assembled a sampling of their quotes on this subject so that rather than tell you what they are saying, you can see for yourself in their own words how they approach the subject of prophetic accountability. We can begin with Rick Joyner,

> "One of the greatest hazards affecting maturing prophets is the erroneous interpretation of the Old Testament exhortation that if a prophet ever predicted something which did not come to pass he was no longer to be considered a true prophet...The warning was that if this happened, the prophet has been presumptuous and the people were not to fear him. If one predicts something in the name of the Lord and it does not come to pass, he probably has spoken presumptuously and needs to be repented of, but that does not make him a false prophet. No one could step out in the faith required to walk in his calling if he knew that a single mistake could ruin him for life."
>
> *("The Prophetic Ministry."* Rick Joyner. Morningstar Prophetic Newsletter. *Vol. 3, No. 2, Page 2).*

How is it erroneous to interpret Moses to be saying that we are to reject inaccurate prophets? If the church is to provoke Israel to jealousy, as living in the inheritance which has been temporarily suspended from Israel, how could inaccurate prophets possibly provoke the people of Moses to jealousy? Joyner then appeals to Bob Jones' teaching on prophetic accuracy,

> "Bob [Jones] was told that the general level of prophetic revelation in the church was about 65% accurate at this time. Some are only about 10% accurate, a very few of the most mature prophets are approaching 85% to 95% accuracy. Prophecy is increasing in purity, but there is a still a long way to go for those who walk in this ministry. This is actually grace for the church now, because 100% accuracy in this ministry would bring a level of accountability to the church which she is too immature to bear at this time. It would result in too many Annaniases and Sapphiras." (Ibid).

Where do we begin to comment on this kind of reasoning? Lets start with the evolutionary view of prophets. It is "maturing" prophets that are being spoken of, who as they mature, evolve or grow into an increasing level of accuracy. Prophecy itself is evolving, "increasing in purity!" It is a good thing too! For if we were presently at the 100% level, there would be corpses all over churches around the World! Think Ananias and Sapphira! Accepting this kind of thinking would actually makes you grateful for inaccurate prophecy, as if it is a blessing! Ananias and Sapphira are used over and over again to make people glad that we aren't quite at the 100% level yet. "100% accuracy in this ministry would bring a level of accountability to the church which she is too immature to bear at this time," isn't that nice? These earnest men want to be accurate, and probably would be, but it is the church which holds it all back, for she is not quite "there yet." One must admit, these people are good at communication!

If the church isn't mature enough, at this time, for 100% prophecy, why didn't that stop God in the book of Acts when Ananias and Sapphira actually did die? Was Israel more mature than we are now, in the days of Isaiah, Jeremiah and Ezekiel? Where are Peter's 30% prophecies or Agabus' 45% prophecies? What other prophets had been given the luxury to grow into 100% accuracy?

Another evasion is in the oft used disclaimer that, "We aren't saying that we are prophets, we are only saying that we have a prophetic ministry." Mike Bickle, for example, in an interview in the book, *Some Said It Thundered*, which is a positive account of the Kansas City Prophets, is asked the question by the author David Pytches, "Do prophets ever get things wrong?"

> "Mike Bickle was at pains to stress that he saw a real distinction between the recognized office of a prophet and those who received revelations and gave prophecies. At KCF they only actually regard Paul Cain as a prophet...though the self effacing Paul would never claim such an office for himself...We asked tactfully if any of them was ever wrong. They all agreed that they had occasionally been proved wrong. Sometimes their revelation was right but their interpretation or application was wrong."
> (*Some Said It Thundered. Pytches. Page 108-109*).

In my opinion, this amounts to a semantical evasion of the Deuteronomy tests. That somehow it's all right to stand up in the name of the Lord, and speak unto God's people, fully expecting to be received as authoritative, as long as you don't call yourself a prophet. Act like a prophet, tell the church you saw Jesus Christ in a vision and a dream, pass on to you the unique and intriguing "words" that this "Jesus" gave you, but when you are proven false, duck out of accountability by denying that you are technically a prophet! It would be different if these people were merely sharing their "insights" of scripture, for then there would be room for debate and discussion. They may, or may not have the correct insights. But these are not mere insights, these are interactive visions, talking angels, authoritative words, predictions etc! In many cases, we are cautioned that to reject these ministries, is to endanger yourself to be another Ananias and Sapphira! These people speak out of both sides of their mouths, on the one hand, they allow themselves to be called prophets, they write books about the coming restoration of prophets, they posture themselves as prophets along the line of an Isaiah or a Daniel, they make excuses for "maturing prophets," but when godly people want to apply valid scriptural tests to them, they deny being a prophet!

Branham, their mentor, did much the same thing. We see this in an excerpt from a book entitled *The Healer Prophet, William Marrion Branham* (author unknown),

"Until the twilight of his ministry, Branham consistently denied that he was a prophet. When informed that he claimed the identity of a prophet while under the anointing, Branham responded, 'You've heard me never as far as speaking I'd say, 'God made me his prophet.' I've heard people say on tape that they picked it up when the inspiration was on, but that was him speaking, not me, see. Better for Him to tell you then for me to tell you that. See?'"

In other words, "I never said I was a prophet, but if I did it wasn't me, it was spoken under the anointing, it was Jesus that called me a prophet!"

Al Dager in his *Media Spotlight Report* on the Kansas City Prophets, in 1990, states,

"Though these men have come to be recognized as prophets by some, Mike Bickle states that he does not recognize them as prophets in the truest sense of the word, but rather as men who have merely been gifted with a prophetic ministry: 'There's no one in our midst that we give the title 'prophet.' The only one I would feel comfortable giving that office would be Paul Cain, but he refuses to accept it. So I'd say both of them-apostle and Prophet-I believe that in God's purpose they exist, but we're very hesitant to designate somebody as being one at this point in time. But I believe that will be recognized in the future...I don't think that the men should go very heavy on calling themselves that; we definitely don't call the other prophetic guys prophets. I don't feel they have the stature of a prophet yet; I think they have a prophetic ministry, but I don't think they are actually at the level of a prophet.'"

Dager went on to say that despite his denials, Bickle had indeed been well documented as calling these men "prophets," and that it is a fallacy to try to separate the prophetic ministry from the office of a prophet,

"Every believer has a 'prophetic ministry,' because we all may receive a word from the Lord, usually a scripture to reprove, rebuke, exhort, or encourage one another. But this is not what these men practice; they claim a prophetic ministry similar to the Old Testament prophets: revealed knowledge gained from direct face to face encounters with God; they give directive prophecies to individuals, entire congregations, and to the church at large. They want the glory of a prophet, but not the responsibility." (Media Spotlight Special Report, Latter Day Prophets.
By Al Dager. PO Box 290, Redmond, Washington 9807-30290).

Not all deny the title in their evasion of prophetic accountability, many just come right out and contradict Moses, as being applicable to a New Testament prophet,
"The prophet who misses it occasionally in his prophecies may be ignorant, immature, or presumptuous, or he may be

ministering with too much zeal and too little wisdom and anointing. But this does not prove him a false prophet...it is certainly possible for a true prophet to be inaccurate. He would not do it knowingly, for a true prophet is so conscientious he would rather never speak at all than speak even one false word or give wrong direction to even one person. So we must understand the distinction between a false prophecy and a false prophet if we are to be open to what God says. One of the quickest ways to get into trouble with God is to accuse one of Christ's prophets falsely. When we do that, we are touching the very nerve of heaven, and we are sure to receive a very negative reaction. God says in His word, 'Do my prophets no harm.' "

*(Bill Hamon. **Prophets and Personal Prophecy**).*

Note that Hamon would remove the objective test of true and false prophets, and would have us test on an entirely subjective level, the prophet's motive. "A true prophet would not do it knowingly." Therefore, even if there are false and misleading prophecies, we are warned not to make a judgement, unless we can determine whether or not it was done knowingly. I doubt that Edgar Cayce "knowingly" was a false prophet, the same goes for Jean Dixon and Nostradamus! It is impossible for us to discern the motives, it isn't within our power or our responsibility, that is why we aren't given such a test in the Old and New Testament.

The extent of this reconditioning of God's people to be more tolerant and accepting of false prophecy on the basis of motive, is illustrated in an editorial article in *Charisma* Magazine in December, 1994, entitled "When Prophecies Prove False," by Karen Howe. The article was in response to the disillusionment many had felt, after believing the aforementioned June 9, 1994 prediction which John Hinkle had proclaimed on TBN, that on that date God would "Rip all evil off of the face of the earth." The author of the article held that the prediction seemed credible because it was verified by "two men with reliable ministries." Howe writes,

"Those of us who were stirred by the words of these men felt a strange mixture of grief (for the poor prophets), embarrassment

65

(at being so gullible ourselves), disappointment (that we couldn't have the announced visitation from God), and frustration (because it's so hard to tell counterfeit gifts from authentic ones). It was especially discomforting for those of us foolish enough to share the prophecies with skeptical non-Christians...And I was once more, angry with God. This would not have happened, I decided, if He had either protected His prophets from false visions or had cooperated by fulfilling their words."

That this article should even have been taken seriously enough to be printed ought to be a wake up call that we in the Charismatic church have been so conditioned against critical thinking, we side more with false prophets than we do with the Honor of God! That anybody would actually consider the use of such an obviously false prediction to evangelize their skeptical friends, is staggering! Another staggering thought is that the "poor prophets" are lauded and the anger was reserved for God, who failed to bail them out! Small wonder we are awash in false prophets! Not to worry though, for the same article explains how the Holy Spirit gave the author a positive way to look at false prophecy, which included, that it was wrong to be mad at God when a human vessel fails. Also to see that in some cases, false prophecies are a temptation from Satan. But were the prophets false? Howe again,

"I believe that the prophets who spoke this year were motivated by courage and caring, not by a desire to deceive. We should pray that their ministries will not suffer, and that the church's gifts of discernment and discretion will be strengthened against further mistakes."

This incredible article concludes by comparing the experience of the false prophecy of 1994, with the crucifixion of Jesus, who on the cross,

"Experienced the seeming contradiction of being abandoned by a God whose nature is to love, not to punish, to support his children, not turn away from them."

There will be a tremendous price paid for our lack of loyalty to God and His word, in fact it is already being paid by many who have submitted their lives to these new prophets. Jack Deere, in a teaching on prophetic ministry at the Toronto Airport Vineyard in November, 1994, acknowledged some of the pitfalls and reservations pastors have to opening their pulpits to "maturing prophets,"

> "Who in the world would be against that ministry? They don't want it in their churches because it causes messes... [begins to describe the experience of one young prophet in training] 'He's standing before a group of high school kids. And he starts out...and he's humbled, and he's a little frightened and kind of awed at the responsibility and he starts calling people out of the audience. And he starts getting it right and the people start oohing and aaahing, and his chest started coming out like this,and you see this garment of pride coming down, and then he calls out a young man of 18 or 19, and he says, 'You're into pornography, and the Lord says you have to repent.' The young man begins to cry. Sits back down. The only problem was the young man wasn't into pornography. He was publically humiliated before 800 high school kids. We had to go back to his church, apologize to his whole church... it was a horrible mess... But do you know what? God is in the process of offending our minds in order to reveal our hearts! And I don't know anyplace where He's going to give us a pure ministry. I don't know anyplace where it's going to be 100% right. There's going to be stumbling blocks in any ministry that the Holy Spirit is really responsible for."

It is amazing that after recounting that horror story of a blatant abuse of so-called prophecy, Deere's conclusion was the tired old mantra, popularized by John Wimber, "God is in the process of offending our minds to reveal our hearts!!" As in the *Charisma* article mentioned earlier, which defended the false prophet who gave the June 9th prophecy, another travesty is perpetrated on the Body of Christ, and the conclusion is that God is responsible for it. God is not libeling 18 year old boys, accusing them of things they haven't done. Not the God of the Bible. "Let us go after other gods which we have not known, and serve them..."

I assure you that with a mind set like this which can justify such abuse of people in the name of "the prophetic," we will have to see a lot more of this, probably even going beyond false testimony against individuals, whole churches will be attacked this way, as long as these false prophets are allowed to continue "maturing" their gift on real people. The damage will prove to be incalculable, in terms of shipwrecked believers, false converts, division in the Body, squandered opportunities to witness, and even wrecked churches. The refusal of our leadership, especially the Pentecostals, to rise up and rebuke this unfaithfulness, will be answerable before the throne of God. Instead of laughing and mourning, we should be weeping! Alas, the scripture in Jeremiah 5 has come to pass in our day, "The prophets prophesy falsely, and the priests bear rule by their means and my people love to have it so." God's people love it. They must love the idea of a "God's Bartender," a seer, who can serve them up personal and self gratifying "words." It is nice to think that our generation is so special, that the apostles in heaven are lined up waiting to shake hands with our latter day apostles. These prophets have appealed to the vanity of a vain generation. The only Spirit they manifest is the Zeitgeist, the spirit of this vanishing age. This is particularly seen in their insistence that there should be no objective tests for them, no absolute by which to test their boastful claims, and that nothing or no one is wrong except those who dare challenge them by the Word of God! In many ways these are postmodern prophets, they don't speak for God, as Jude says, "these be they who separate themselves, they are sensual, having not the Spirit."

The justifications for false and inaccurate prophecies are endless, for there is a constant need for them. One of the most creative I've seen was given by Bob Jones, in an interview with Mike Bickle, on the widely distributed tape, "The Shepherd's Rod,"

[Jones] "The Rhema will be two thirds right on. Not quite time for Ananias and Sapphira yet"
[Bickle] "The Lord actually said that sentence to you?"
[Jones] "Yeah, I mean what he was really showing me was, 'I'm

going to release the Rhema to where that many begin to move two-thirds right on with their words, and the other third will be like poppin' a bullet at the enemy and He wouldn't fire. It was a blank'. And He [God] said, 'I'm the one that's loading the gun, so there's going to be some blanks there...the blanks is pointed in the general direction of the enemy anyway'...'If I [God] release the 100% Rhema right now, the accountability would be so awesome and you'd have so much Ananias and Sapphira's going on the people couldn't grow.'"

This is an amazing statement, which makes God responsible for the "blanks" (false prophecies) and gives Him a reason for deceiving us! He would actually make you feel relieved and thankful for false prophecy, using the old Ananias and Sapphira threat. We must be a special generation, we are the first one ever, that God supposedly protected from His 100% accurate Word! To this day, Bickle, the Vineyard and many others involved, consider Jones to be a "Man with a very profound prophetic ministry." (*Growing in the Prophetic.* Mike Bickle. Creation House.) The closest Bickle came to it, was by stating that Jones never should have been put on the front stage, he should have been allowed to be some kind of a "backstage" prophet. (See my book *Weighed and Found Wanting* for a fuller treatment of this false prophet).

What is going to become of us Pentecostals? Whether we know it or not, Satan has desired to have us that he may sift us as wheat (Luke 22:31). We are currently being tested for our love of God, our loyalty, and that love is as God defines it. If our Lord will have mercy on us, He will sober us up, for the times definitely don't call for spiritual drunkenness. We need to have clear heads for clear, biblical thinking, it has become a matter of loyalty to God. And for full spiritual life, true spirituality. We don't have to chose between "Charismania" or deadness. It is just as sinful for the orthodox remnant of the church to have no passion for God, no life of worship, no love of people, as it is for the other side of the church to be so opened to everything coming down the road.

As the psalmist cried out, "Who will rise up for me against the evildoers?" Will we shepherds ever be faithful and protect our flocks, regain our convictions and quit taking our signals from the most current religious fad? Will we be willing to be obscure, and toil thanklessly in the Lord's fields, or do we insist on being "with it?" I am no prophet, but I will close for now with a prophecy.

"I will gather the remnant of my flock out of all countries whither I have driven them, and will bring them again to their folds, and they shall be fruitful and increase, and I will set up shepherds over them which shall feed them, and they shall fear no more, nor be dismayed, neither shall they be lacking, saith the Lord...And I will give you pastors according to my own heart which shall feed you with knowledge and understanding." (Jeremiah 3 and 23).

Chapter Nine

Why God Holds Pastors Responsible

"A wonderful and horrible thing is committed in the land; The prophets prophesy falsely, and the priests bear rule by their means; and my people love to have it so: and what will ye do in the end thereof?" Jeremiah 5:30-31.

> "I think you'll find that the prophets are pretty nice people, by and large. I've come to know them and love them. We've invited several of them here, I think maybe five or six, that are from the Kansas City Fellowship. And then we have Paul Cain..."
>
> *(John Wimber, "Unpacking Your Bags," audio tape)*

Jeremiah 23 is a polemic against false prophets, which starts out by putting the blame where it really belongs. Who does the Lord make responsible for the explosion of false prophets, initially? Not the false prophets, nor the congregations, but the Pastors! God knows that the ministries of these false prophets would be all but impossible without pastors opening up their platforms and pulpits to them.

"Woe be unto the Pastors that destroy and scatter the sheep of my pasture, saith the Lord. Therefore thus saith the Lord God of Israel against the pastors that feed my people; Ye have scattered my flock, and driven them away, and have not visited them: behold, I will visit upon you the evil of your doings, saith the Lord." (Jeremiah 23:12)

How would these false prophets even exist without shepherds opening up their pulpits to give them meetings? Therefore it is the shepherds that God addresses when He opens up this passage about false prophets. Pastors are supposed to feed their sheep the Word of God, and protect them from wolves. The flourishing of false prophets, is an indictment against us for

71

failing to faithfully do this! The Word of God, like manna, has failed to satisfy the lust too many have for the novel and exciting! A good number of us shepherds are going to have to answer to charges that for gain, and out of greed, or fear of being left out, we have opened our flocks to the teachings and prophecies of these men who speak such great swelling words of great vanity.

The current false movements have succeeded in creating an incredible peer pressure in the ministry. The pressure is on to distinguish yourself as a church which is "cutting edge," spot on with the latest of the current religious fads. The last thing anyone would want to be accused of is being "dead" or "religious." Thus a good many Pastors are "desperate," but it is not the desperation that pushes an individual to seek God. The kind of desperation many pastors are experiencing these days, is the desperation to keep up with the fast moving trends in the religious world of today. "If we don't open up to the Pensacola revival, the church down the road just may, and I'll lose half of my people." This desperation never leads one to fasting and prayer, but rather to conferences and church growth seminars. When asked about why he plunged his church into Toronto, in spite of his admitted reservations, one pastor candidly replied,

> "I wasn't sure if it was of God or not, but we were so dry, and so desperate we couldn't afford not to take the chance..."

Results. Truth is secondary these days, just give us some results, generate some excitement, or we will scatter in this wilderness. Hirelings are defined as those who run, when the wolf comes, rather than lay down their lives to protect God's sheep. Who are the modern hirelings? The ones who know that these new religious fads are unscriptural, but are afraid of standing up to them, lest they lose their numbers, prestige, "anointed" reputation, and so forth. Like Aaron in the golden calf incident, they know this is wrong, but in order not to scatter the people, they are willing to offer them something to see, feel, and experience. They don't advocate a new God, but they inaugurate ways of worshiping Him, and "points of contact" to Him that He Himself has never instituted. This is called "Will Worship" in the scriptures, the worship of God on our own terms. As in the Golden Calf incident, they have proclaimed a "feast unto Jahweh" where there is no feast! (Exodus 32:5).

There are a lot of Aarons these days in Pentecostal and Charismatic leadership, who know that these movements are wrong; Toronto Blessing, Pensacola, Promise Keepers, Drunkenness in the Spirit, and Ecumenism, but they are afraid of losing their lives and ministries for truth, so they compromise. Beside that, it is so profitable to cater to recent religious fads. When Aaron took an offering for the Golden Calf, it was one of the most willing offerings ever taken, for people will gladly pay for their idols,

"And Aaron said unto them, break off the golden earrings, which are in the ears of your wives, of your sons, and of your daughters, and bring them unto me, and all the people brake off the golden earrings which were in their ears and brought them unto Aaron." *(Exodus 32:23).*

The Assemblies of God are an example of this, for they condemned Toronto, and the laughing revival, until they had their own version of it. What is the difference between Toronto and Pensacola? One gave birth to the other. Pensacola sprang from the Holy Trinity Brompton Church in London England, the church which virtually blanketed England with the Toronto Blessing, and which literally coined the phrase, Toronto Blessing. Can both good and bad water come from the same source? (see Appendix I). How the Assemblies of God could have shone brightly these days, holding up the truth of the Gospel! There are many independent Pentecostals who have looked up to the Assemblies, because of their previous strength, experience, and holiness. I have no doubt that there are still many within the denomination who are grieved over the apostasy, but the leadership seems to have taken the "ends justify the means" approach. These new revivals are appealing because they do generate excitement!

Going back to Jeremiah 23. It is because of the hireling mentality of the shepherds, the Pastors, that the people of God were affected by the prophets. And what are those effects?

Folly and Error

"I have seen folly in the prophets of Samaria...They have caused my people Israel to err..." (Jeremiah 23:13).

There are numerous examples of the folly and error that false prophets have brought upon God's people. Jacob Prasch tells of the British Prophet, Gerald Coates (see Appendix 4) who foretold of an earthquake in New Zealand, which persuaded the leaders of a Pentecostal denomination to appear on national television there, to warn the nation. The national news coverage leading up to it featured churches taking survival courses, on the basis of that prophetic "word." When the predicted date came and went, the Christian church was made into a national laughing-stock. A sincere, but naive Christian leader was made a fool of in his own nation, all because he allowed himself and many to listen to a false prophet's predictions.

Profaneness
"...For from the prophets of Jerusalem is profaneness gone forth into all the land..."
(Jeremiah 23:15).

Do you know what the word Profaneness means? To profane something means to make it into something common, nothing special at all. It is the opposite of the word holy, or sacred, which means special, set apart. God's Word is Holy, special and set apart. It is to be regarded as Holy by His people. When Christians, who have been bought with the blood of the Lamb, and have received the Holy Spirit, and been exposed to the Bible feel they then need to go out, crossing land and sea, to get a "word from the Lord," through people like the Kansas City Prophets, they are profaning the Holy Word of God. The Word of God is being profaned by those who are constantly saying things like, "God is a lot more than God the Father, God the Son, and God the Holy Book" or "God is a lot bigger than a doctrine" or even "The church is so hung up on "bible study" they don't really know Jesus." These are the same people who produce reams and reams of prophecies, expecting you to take those seriously! This profanity will spill out into other areas for it cannot long be contained. I believe that the

74

prophecy movement is partly responsible for a kind of "been there, done that"attitude to the teaching and preaching of the Word of God.

They Make You Vain!

"Thus saith the Lord of Hosts, hearken not to the words of the prophets that prophesy unto you: they make you vain: they speak a vision of their own heart, and not out of the mouth of the Lord." (Jeremiah 23:16)

The false prophets will make you vain! This is the warning of Jeremiah, to those who would be enamored of these new Seers. In biblical thought, vanity is a blight to be avoided, for it means "lightness," irrelevancy, to be futile and of no consequence.

Think about it; we live in a world that is in spiritual and moral confusion, and a good many thinking people are aware of this, both saved and unsaved. At a time when the Christian church could be holding forth substantial answers, that actually speak to the current dilemma of man; answers that are a part of our inheritance from Christ, we are instead being seduced into abandonment of our thinking faculties, by the Rodney Howard Browne's of this world, who beckon us to "turn off your mind and go with the flow." This false prophetic movement has made us vain! It has promised renewal to countless thousands of Pastors and churches, but it has instead tended toward self absorption. That shouldn't surprise us when you consider the content of the bulk of these prophecies. They fall into the categories of either the, "You are the greatest generation of the church ever" variety, or more along the lines of an "Annanias and Sapphira are the fate of those who dare question this movement" type of utterance. After twenty years or more of this, anyone would be vain. Pastors, we are responsible for this; Why have we opened the flocks up to this? What were we looking for when we sought these ministries? We have succeeded in making our people vain, when they could be sharp, sober and ready, able to give an answer for the hope we have in Christ, instead of being self absorbed, drunk in the spirit, living for the next 'outpouring'.

I warned in my earlier book, *Weighed and Found Wanting: Putting the Toronto Blessing in Context*, that spiritual drunkenness is real, but it is not a blessing from God, but rather a judgement on an unfaithful and unbelieving church! Isaiah proclaims,

"His watchmen are blind: they are all ignorant, they are all dumb dogs, they cannot bark, sleeping, lying down, loving to slumber, Yea, they are greedy dogs which can never have enough, and they are shepherds that cannot understand: they all look to their own way, everyone for his gain, from his quarter, Come ye, say they, I will fetch wine and we will fill ourselves with strong drink, and tomorrow shall be as today, and much more abundant." (Isaiah 56:1012)

They Encourage Them That Despise the Lord
"They say unto them that despise me, The Lord hath said Ye shall have peace; and they say unto every one that walketh in the imagination of his own heart, No evil shall come upon you." (Jeremiah 23:17).

There is a tremendous judgement coming upon our nation for her many sins, and of course judgement must begin in the house of God, for as Peter has rightly said, "If the righteous scarcely be saved, what will become of the ungodly and the sinners?" (I Peter 4:18). Peter and the apostles called the church to soberness, vigilance, good works, and so forth in view of the coming day of God's judgement,

"Seeing then that all these things shall be dissolved, what manner of persons ought you to be, in all holy conversation and godliness, looking for and hastening unto the coming day of God." (2 Peter 3:11-12).

Those who despise the Lord are not necessarily those who hate the Lord, for in biblical usage, to despise is to esteem lightly, to fail to take a person seriously. The new prophets are dangerous, because they make the church the issue and not the Lord. Their prophecies, as I have already demonstrated, are about the coming greatness of the church, what we will do, how we will reign, our exploits (of course, "in the power of God"). The actual bodily return of Jesus is not the true goal of the new prophets, in many cases, rather it is the coming glory, the "presence of God" that has been prophesied by these, to envelope the church, in the days immediately preceding the bodily return of Jesus. Instead of calling men to "Fear God and give glory to Him, for the hour of His judgement has come." (Revelation 14:7) An indulgent church is being urged to "soak" up as much of the "anointing" as possible, to get drunk on the New Wine, and to enlist themselves into Joel's Army, an army that itself is doomed to be judged by God! (Joel 2:20).

They encourage them who despise the Lord to carry on in a thousand and one ways! For example, if a man really fears the Lord, he will want to exercise discernment, to think critically, and to not just throw open his spirit to every passing religious fad. These new prophets strongly discourage this, to the point of mockery and threatenings! They have helped to foster an antagonism in the church, between the ones that they have seduced, and those who are more cautious. The "Civil War" prophecy of Joyner, Campbell, Bob Jones, and James Ryle, the sarcasm of Rodney Howard Browne (rarely missing an opportunity to mock and castigate his detractors), the whole "us/them" mentality, has given much encouragement to those who despise the Lord enough to relish this division.

"But if they had stood in my council and had caused my people to hear my words, then they should have turned them from their evil ways, and from the evil of their doings." (Jeremiah 23:22).

In conclusion, the Pastors have been given the charge to feed and protect the Flock of God, which He purchased with His own Blood. Therefore, the responsibility for the false prophets in part is laid to rest at their feet. These false prophets would not be able to operate if the people of God had been fed sound doctrine, and if the Shepherds were willing to Bark! Therefore the chapter in Jeremiah that explicitly discusses False Prophets, begins with, "Woe to the Pastors..." (Jeremiah 23:1). In the very face of false predictions, outrageous teaching and glaring misuse of spiritual gifts, too many Pastors insist that all of that can be overlooked for the potential benefits that these false prophets offer.

Chapter 10

The Distinguishing Marks of a False Prophet

"We should not judge Bill Clinton solely by how he may appear at this time. We cannot continue to get our discernment from the news Media. The Bill Clinton that the Lord Showed Paul Cain in the dream is different from the media's portrayal of Him. We must start to see people as the Lord sees them... Bill Clinton won and so can we. The reason Paul Cain was shown five headlines in the dream is because Bill Clinton represents grace from God,not judgement..."

> (**Morningstar Prophetic Bulletin**, January, 1993, article by Paul Cain and Rick Joyner)

"Error, indeed, is never set forth in its naked deformity, lest it being thus exposed, it should at once be detected. But it is craftily decked out in an attractive dress, so as, by its outward form, to make it appear to the inexperienced...more true than the truth itself."

> (Irenaeus, **Against Heresies** [Preface 2] c180-190AD)

The time has come for the practical portion of this book. Our burden from the start, has been to provide the believer with the necessary equipment for the exercise of discernment in these times. Especially the pastors, who must contend with this increasing tide of error. We are reminded of two assurances, from our merciful Lord, that "When the enemy comes in like a flood, the Spirit of the Lord will raise up a standard against him," (Isaiah 59:19) and also we are told that by the Knowledge of the Holy Scriptures, "The man of God is perfect, thoroughly furnished unto all good works." (2 Timothy 3:17). With those thoughts in mind, let us take a look at what the Word of God sets forth as the distinguishing Marks of False Prophets.

False Prophets Make False Predictions

The foundational test is laid out in Moses, and it is quite simple; predictions made by false prophets, fail to come to pass.

"And if you say in thine heart, How shall we know the word which the Lord has not spoken? When a prophet speaks in the name of the Lord, if the thing follow not, nor come to pass, that is the thing which the Lord has not spoken, but the prophet hath spoken presumptuously: you shalt not be afraid of Him." (Deuteronomy 18:21-22)

It is truly amazing to me that this simple prescription, given for the safety of God's people is considered inapplicable, on the basis of it being Old Testament. Nowhere in the New Testament, is this simple test invalidated, we are never counseled by Jesus or the Apostles to consider in any sense that those who make inaccurate predictions are to be accepted as prophets of God.

Much of the current confusion we are seeing these days on this point is a result of the inability to distinguish three separate functions of Prophetic grace. There are first Old Testament Prophets, then New testament Prophets and finally those used in the utterance gifts of the Spirit.

All basically agree that the Old Testament Prophets, such as Isaiah, Jeremiah, and Ezekiel, fall under the Deuteronomy 18 test. Not one Old Testament Prophet could be inaccurate, not even in 1% of their prophetic utterances!

Concerning the third category, those used in the utterance gifts of the Spirit; prophesying for "edification, exhortation, and comfort" (I Corinthians 14:3), are not in the same category as those who call themselves prophets. Any Christian may potentially be given a prophetic utterance, (I Corinthians 14:31). But to be used in that gift is not the same as being a Prophet. Acts 21 brings out this distinction, in verses 9-10,

"And the same man had four daughters, virgins, which did prophesy, and as we tarried there many days, there came down from Judea a certain prophet named Agabus."

The new prophets don't claim to merely give prophecies, rather they are "moving in a Prophetic anointing." They have conversations with Angels,

God, Demons, they dream interactive dreams, they make proclamations in the name of the Lord, they have been to heaven. They make pronouncements to the whole church! In reality, they consider themselves prophets in the sense of Isaiah and Jeremiah, which is fine, as long as they are willing to submit to the same test, for the church's sake.

As we have already demonstrated, the contention is that inaccuracy is allowed in New Testament times, for "immature," prophets are allowed now to "develop" their gifts! It amounts to an almost evolutionary view of prophets, still "growing into 100% accuracy."

Much is made of I Corinthians 14:28, "Let the prophets speak two or three, and let the other judge." This passage is simply telling us that prophecy is to be judged. Paul is saying the same thing that Moses says in Deuteronomy 18, and 13. The difference now is that the church is not a Theocratic nation State as Israel was, and has no option of capital punishment, we don't stone false prophets. On the other hand there is no indication that we should allow the ministry of inaccurate prophets to be received either. The penalty for false prophecy is lessened in a temporal sense, but the seriousness of it hasn't.

We can see in the Book of Acts, that there were New Testament Prophets, who seemed to operate in the same sense as Old Testament Prophets, Agabus, for example. It is helpful to note that his prophecies were always validated by God. I have yet to be shown even one New Testament prophet who made inaccurate prophecies!

As for the prophets we have dealt with in this book, the inaccuracies made in the name of the Lord are numerous! We have already mentioned the much heralded prophecy that "all evil would be ripped off of the face of the earth on June 9, 1994," which came and went without much stir. In early 1993, Rick Joyner and Paul Cain both had optimistic things to say about Bill Clinton. Cain was shown five headlines in a dream, because, five is the number of grace,

"Bill Clinton represents grace from God, not judgement...In the dream Paul was told that Bill Clinton was better than what we deserved, and that he may be viewed as the best president in America since Dwight Eisenhower...The Lord wants to use Bill

Clinton to move the country forward and not backward."
(*Morningstar Prophetic Bulletin*, January 1993)

Here we are, six years later, in 1999. What Spirit told these men to proclaim these things?

The same Spirit told Cain and Joyner that Clinton represents a "Reprieve from a New World Order that the church is not prepared to face at this time." The whole Clinton Presidency has been nothing but an advancement of the policies of the New World Order! This prediction has failed to come to pass, putting the validity of these "prophets" in question.

False Prophets Have False Doctrine

When considering any prophets, we have to not allow ourselves to be sidetracked by the miracles, signs and wonders, even the predictions, for none of these are central to the essence of prophetic ministry. All prophets, true or false, bring a message. The signs and wonders, if there are any, only serve to validate that message, they are not ends in themselves! (The reason I say, "if there are any" signs and wonders, is because the "greatest prophet ever born of a woman," John The Baptist, did no miracles!) Miracles and wonders and predictions are not essential to prophetic ministry, the message of the prophet is.

Isaiah and Jeremiah didn't go around giving people personal Words at meetings! Neither did John Baptist or Agabus. Moses didn't throw his cloak at crowds to see them slain in the Spirit. These people were first of all Preachers and Teachers! In the process of giving their messages, which called Israel back to the Law of Moses and the nations unto God in repentance, and warned both of coming judgements, they did indeed often make predictions, and effect healings. But what they were truly about was what they referred to as "their burden," "the Word of the Lord" which came unto them speaking; their text was the Holy Scripture,

This is why Moses warned us in Deuteronomy 13, and John in I John 4, that when "Testing the Spirits" of prophets or ministries, it is not enough to know that so and so was healed, or that this or that family was brought together, for even the Mormons have produced that much. The true issue is always, "What is the content of the message?" If prophets are preachers and

81

Teachers, it follows that False prophets are false teachers! Peter makes this connection in 2 Peter 2:1.

"But there were false prophets also among the people, even as there shall be false teachers among you, who privily shall bring in damnable heresies, even denying the Lord who bought them, and bring upon themselves swift destruction..."

The thought conveyed in the Greek is that they shall subtly lay lies along side of truth in such a way that the two are all but indistinguishable. There are many "good" things being said by many of these teachers and preachers. But we have to remember that rat poison is 95% nutritious!

This is why Jesus told us in Matthew 12:35 that the fruit of a prophet, is his Words, for "By thy Words thou shalt be justified and by thy Words thou shalt be condemned." This is no different than Moses' warning of the Prophet or dreamer of dreams, whose prediction may well have appeared to come to pass, but whose consistent message is a form of "let us go after other gods, which we have not known, to serve them," or John's warning, that "Any Spirit that confesseth not, that Jesus Christ came in the flesh, is the Spirit of Anti Christ." All are agreed, the test of a prophet is his or her doctrine. False prophets are off, because their doctrines are off. Of these there are myriad examples. Jewel Van Der Merwe recounts one such example in her *Discernment* magazine, of March 1993,

> "On February 25, 1993, a 'prophet' was on TBN with Matt Crouch, the son of Paul and Jan...On this particular broadcast it was taught that the Body of Christ doesn't understand what the prophet really is. They just don't understand that the Old Testament Prophet was different from the New Testament prophet. Naturally they would say that!...the way a prophet is defined today makes him not responsible for his prophecies! All the responsibility falls upon the person to whom the prophecy is given! If the prophecy doesn't come to pass, it is that person's fault...The new prophets are claiming their utterances are...literally the UTTERANCE OF GOD...the "spoken Word"...the "Fresh Word from God." This word is on a par with, and in some instances above the written Word.

Their claim is that the "spoken word" actually makes the "prophet" a partaker of the DIVINE NATURE...On the TBN program, this particular "prophet" Kim Clement, actually said that the Christians will be a superhuman powerful force that will grind Satan into the ground. The very topping on the cake was that the Word of God when used was twisted. For example, Matthew 16:1618, "Peter ...said, Thou art Christ, the Son of the Living God. And Jesus...said...flesh and blood has not revealed it unto thee, but my Father which is in heaven...and upon this rock I will build my church; and the gates of Hell will not prevail against it."...This scripture was interpreted on this program as meaning, "Christians must get into revelation from the Word." Yes this sounds very good. However it is how "the Word" is defined that is so troubling. By the "Word," this "prophet" means a fresh prophetic voice, or revelation experienced subjectively apart from the literal Bible revelation. He intimated that for Christians to survive they must build on new subjective revelations and experiences. This concept makes the written Word of God of no effect, especially if this new revelation is put on a par with scripture...So the Prophet continues "...and upon this rock of revelation, I will build my church. There has to be a fresh revelation for the church today to built on, and the Gates of Hell will not prevail against the rock of this fresh revelation!"...Matt Crouch's enthusiastic response was, "The Word that we heard as children is not fresh revelation and is not applicable for today. It isn't any good for the warfare today...we are building on Christ and Fresh revelation."

(Discernment, *March/April, 1993, "Prophets, Etc." by Jewel van Der Merwe).*

If Matt Crouch "got it," so did the thousands of television viewers who happened to be tuned in that day to receive ministry from the TBN Prophet. But what did they "get?" They seemed to be getting the same thing that Eve got, when she listened to that long, skinny Prophet, coiled around the Tree of the knowledge of Good and Evil. "Has God said?" In other words, "the Word that we heard as children is not fresh...no longer applicable for today." No amount of accurate predictions, conversions, healings or apparent miracles should induce a Child of God to accept such a ministry, after hearing that kind of teaching.

False Prophets Hate to Be Tested

Jeremiah was a true prophet, who ministered in the final days of the Kingdom of Judah, immediately before the Babylonian captivity. Another Prophet named Hananiah, was far more popular in the Land of Judah. His name means, God has been Gracious. Names can be deceiving. False prophets usually come across as gracious and humble, initially, but sooner or later, their dark side comes out.

God had instructed Jeremiah to wear a yoke of bondage, as a sign of the coming captivity. Hananiah came forth with an utterance, to Jeremiah in the temple, in front of all of the priests and people, saying,

"Thus saith the Lord of Hosts, the God of Israel saying,'I have broken the yoke of the king of Babylon. Within two full years will I bring again into this place all the vessels of the Lord's house." (Jeremiah 28:1)

Hananiah prophesied the opposite of what Jeremiah the Prophet had been warning of, in the temple, in the presence of the priests! Jeremiah's response was that he would love for Hananiah's prophecy to be true, but it was in contradiction to all of the previous prophets, to prophesy SHALOM (Peace, all is well) when the nation was sinful and unrepentant. At this point Hananiah suddenly lost his gracious and humble composure, for he walked up to Jeremiah, took off of him the yoke that the Lord had told him to wear, and broke it!

"Then said the prophet Jeremiah unto Hananiah the prophet, Hear now Hananiah; The Lord hath not sent thee, but thou makest these people to trust in a lie. Therefore thus saith the Lord, Behold I will cast thee off from the face of the earth: this year you will die, because you have taught rebellion against the Lord." (Jeremiah 28:15-16)

84

True prophets don't mind scrutiny, as long as they are being measured by the standard of the Word of God, False prophets resent it and castigate those who would dare appeal to the standard of judgement, as being "religious," judgmental, "fearful," and reactionary. Those who refuse to exercise discernment are applauded as being "open to God."

False Prophets Are Man Centered

"Woe to you when all men speak well of you, for so did their Fathers to the false prophets..." (Luke 6:26)

False prophets are about Man. Here again from the above quoted article by Jewel Van Der Merwe,

> "[P]ositive prophecies also came out on the TBN program with Kim Clement and Matt Crouch. Kim said he was tired of "so-called prophets" saying that this country was going to be judged. He didn't think this country would be judged because they send out so many missionaries. Instead, he believed that tremendous blessing was coming on America. In fact, he stated that the body of Christ is becoming very aggressive, songs becoming militant, and the church is getting ready to fight. In fact if you prophesy "doom and gloom" you are not going to be a part of what God is going to do! He was prophesying that there is going to be an incredible breakthrough and revival in twenty months."
>
> **(Discernment)**

Kim Clement is a man widely acclaimed as a prophet! A full page ad in *Charisma* magazine heralded his meetings in Detroit, with the announcement, "The Light has come to Detroit!" and a quote from one of his prophecies. Who wouldn't want incredible blessing to come upon America? Peter and Jude both warn of those who would come along speaking "great swelling words, having men's persons in admiration because of advantage." (Jude 16)

False Prophets Can Be Accurate in Their Signs

Just because a prophet has a few miracles, it doesn't mean he is of God. Mormonism began with the working of a number of apparent miracles, Roman Catholicism has its miracles also. The Word of God warns us that in the last days the truth will be withstood by men like Jannes and Jambres. *"Now as Jannes and Jambres withstood Moses, so do these also resist the truth: men of corrupt minds, reprobate concerning the Faith." (2 Timothy 3:8).*

Jannes and Jambres were the prophets who stood before Pharaoh, and seemed to have "the stuff" in the days of Moses. Up to a point, they could virtually duplicate all of the miracles of Moses. Paul warns us of the time in the Last Days, when the Truth will be resisted by similar miracle workers. He said in another place, that we should be aware of the coming of "Him whose coming is after the working of Satan, with all power and signs and lying wonders, and with all deceivableness of unrighteousness in them that perish; because they received not the love of the truth, for this cause God shall send them strong delusion." (2 Thess 2:911).

It is hard for modern people to imagine that God Himself would actually "send strong delusion" upon us in the Last days. This is admittedly a hard word. But Paul is saying in a New Testament context, what Moses told us,
"If there arise among you a Prophet or a dreamer of dreams, and giveth you a sign or a wonder, And the sign or wonder come to pass, whereof he spake unto you saying, Let us go after other gods, which thou hast not known, and let us serve them; Thou shalt not hearken unto the Words of that Prophet, or that dreamer of dreams, for the Lord your God proveth you, to know whether you Love the Lord your God with all of your heart and all of your soul." (Deuteronomy 13:13).

Therefore we can conclude that it is the Lord, who allows False prophets to flourish at times,and even allows there signs to seem to be valid! And why does He allow this? That he might prove our Love. Do we Love the Lord our God? On a subjective basis, I am convinced that there has never been a time in the history of western civilisation, where more people felt as though they were passionately in Love with God. Never have the songs of praise and adoration and worship, been so intensely emotional, intimate, almost romantic! People are swooning for God, young people are getting drunk in the spirit for God, Love for God is provoking people to literally abandon all of their thinking faculties,in the pursuit of passion for God.

But how does God say we should Love Him? The Word of God makes reference to "will worship," in Colossians 2:23. Will Worship, refers not to the worship of the will, but to the worship of God according to the Human will. God tells us not only to Love him, but even how He is to be Loved. What does it mean to Love God? How does God define Loving God?

The rise of False prophets forces us to confront this issue in our own lives, because to God, Love translates into loyalty. If you love God, then you will be willing to judge and discern prophets, rejecting the ones who bring a false message, in spite of any apparent signs or wonders. All of those who follow the people we have mentioned in this book, are undoubtedly sure that they "Love God!" But to God, the proof of that Love is shown when miracle working, signs and wonders dealing false prophets arise. Loyalty to God is loyalty to the revealed Word of God. Jesus said, "If you Love me you will keep my Word."

We are on the verge of the greatest test any of us have ever been involved in. The steady stream of false Christian ministries have conditioned many of us to accept almost anybody who comes in the name of the Lord. If Christians will accept uncritically the outrageous teachings of a Benny Hinn or a Rodney Howard Browne, what will we do when a demonically inspired deceiver like the AntiChrist comes along? If we can't see through Robert Schuller, the Pope or Mother Teresa, how are we going to withstand the ultimate False Prophet of Revelation 13?

Those who are faithful in little will be given more, and in the Last Days, what is going to be given to the Faithful, is understanding. As Daniel, a real prophet of God said, "And such as do wickedly against the covenant shall he corrupt with flatteries: But the people who know their God shall be strong and do exploits, And they that understand among the people shall instruct many." (Daniel 11:32-33).

Except for the appendixes, I close for now, with this promise, "Now unto Him who is able to keep us from stumbling, and to present you blameless before the presence of His glory with great joy, to the only wise God our Saviour, be glory, majesty, dominion and power, both now and forever. Amen" (Jude 24-25)

Grow in Grace.

Epilogue

They Will Say...

Quo Vadis? Where are we going? We, being the Pentecostal and Charismatic movement, and even the evangelical church of Jesus Christ. There are those who say that we are on the verge of the "Greatest Revival the church has ever known." They confidently assert that the Toronto and Pensacola revivals are on the forefront of the long awaited and much prophesied, "Last days, worldwide revival" that is to sweep whole nations into the Kingdom of God and cause the names of modern prophets and apostles to become known worldwide. "Nations will tremble at the mention of their name," is how one modern day prophet described it.

On the other hand, there are those who see current trends in a more ominous light. Rather than a great last days revival, many are beginning to ask the question that Jesus posed in the Gospel of Luke, "Will the Son of Man find faith when He comes to the earth?" Thus there is a polarization, a parting of the ways among Christians who are equally sincere in their beliefs. Where are we going? Revival or apostasy? I believe that the Gospel of Matthew has something to say to these times in the form of two sayings of the Lord Jesus, who spoke of these in the context of discussion about the last days and the professing church. These statements seem to point to a progression of error, resulting in the apostasy of many. I will give them in the order that they were given and comment on each step of them.

They Will Say to Me Lord, Lord...

The first step in the progression is what I will refer to as an easy believism, a cheapened view of salvation. "Lord, Lord,..." will be the cry of many! In

89

other words, Christianity will be "in." In some way, it will be popular with the masses. And, of course, I think all will agree that we have succeeded in popularizing Christianity to the point where everyone seems to be wearing crosses, Christian artists are being accepted in secular markets, prominent athletes testify publically of conversion experiences. Even the President of the United States seems as comfortable in a Baptist church as in the corridors of power. In one sense, it seems that evangelical Christians have actually succeeded in Christianizing the nation on every level. Thousands of us are saying, "Lord, Lord,..." We know the songs, read the books and partake of the popular Christian culture. Christianity is "in." It's made it. I remember the election of 1976 when Jimmy Carter announced that he was a "Born Again" Christian and the media didn't know what that even meant! A short twenty years later and the words "Born Again" are mainstream, immediately understood by most mainstream people.

But what kind of Christianity have these thousands embraced? Are we as Christian as we think we are? If so, many thousands have been "born again." How do we explain the degeneration of our society, of which it would be redundant for me to describe? There is nothing wrong with saying "Lord, Lord,..." and singing of the Lord and praying to the Lord, as long as He truly has been acknowledged as LORD, the Master, and King! But, the first warning of Jesus in these seven warnings is the warning of false conversion.

There are many who would swear up and down that they are saved, born again, they prayed a prayer, asked Jesus to be their "personal Savior," who aren't actually saved! They will be shocked on that day, that their confidence was misplaced. "Depart from Me, you workers of iniquity." In other words, "You did your own thing!" Iniquity, lawlessness, is the blight of our day, the prevalent sin of our time. And somehow or other, we have reshaped our presentation of the Gospel to lead many to believe that there can be a salvation for those who don't really want to obey the Lord, but want fire insurance.

The antidote to this is to look again at the sermons of the book of Acts. The issues that the Apostles addressed in their evangelism were not the same ones we press these days. We talk often to the sinner about the love of Jesus, and the "wonderful plan" God has for their life. We imply that God is out there waiting for them to just "open up" to Him so that He also, can be a part of their life. Sinners imagine that when they are ready, they can "invite Jesus to be their personal Savior." Small wonder the churches are full of religious consumers, Christians on their own terms who have never imagined that they have to fear God! Not so the evangelism of the Book of Acts! The issues that the apostles emphasised were different, the point was never "invite Jesus to be your personal Savior," nor even "Make Jesus your Lord." How can sinful man "make Jesus Lord?" As Peter Proclaimed in Acts, "God has made this Jesus Lord and Christ whom you have crucified!" Jesus is Lord and God commands you to recognize this! Law, the broken law of God, was discussed first, not love. No one invited Jesus to come in, they were commanded to turn to Him while there was still time! None of this, "He'll always be there waiting for you," instead "Save yourself from this perverted generation!" Jude tells us that "on some, you can have compassion, making a difference," but others must be "saved with fear, pulling them out of the fire hating even the garment spotted by the flesh."

Nonetheless, many say unto Him, "Lord, Lord,..." and are totally unaware of their great danger. But our progression doesn't stay here, it moves on...

Didn't We Prophesy In Thy Name?

False Christians need to be entertained and, like manna, soon the Bible gets, well, old, predictable and boring. For all of those who have heard all of the sermons, over and over again, and yet still yearn for a "Word from the Lord," there has arisen a prophetic movement, which we have attempted to document here. Initially, there is a renewed religious excitement as prophets go forth and tell you what you wanted to hear, but couldn't in "plain old doctrine," that you are part of the greatest generation which ever lived, and that the exploits you will be doing will bring leaders of nations to the Lord. It must be somewhat exhilarating to be called out of a congregation and given your own personal word from God! The excitement and novelty are such that people have been traveling the length and breadth of the globe, to conferences and meetings wherever new anointed prophets are reputed to be.

We can all prophesy, we learn. Techniques are now being taught in prophetic thought, dream interpretation, visualization and allegorical hermeneutics. Major prophetic impartations are being conferred on whole churches, and the decade of the restoration of the prophets has already passed! The prophecies are almost never negative, they always portray the coming "outpouring," the Great Last Days Revival to come, and how great the church will soon be. The only negative pronouncements are towards those who would question this great anointing.

Well, one can only hear so many comforting words, and go to so many conferences, before the novelty wears off, and you have to at least feel like you are doing something useful for God. That's when they will say,

Didn't We Cast Out Devils?

Enter a spiritual warfare movement. We don't just prophesy, nor do we merely receive prophecies. We cast out devils. And like everything else our generation approaches, we don't do it in a run of the mill fashion, casting one low level demon imp out of one lowly person! We really do it on a big scale, we cast demons out of whole cities! I have documented this in my first book, *Making War in the Heavenlies: A Different Look at Spiritual Warfare.* Through the teachings of C. Peter Wagner, Dick Bernal, Francis Frangipane, John Dawson and a host of others, a dualistic Spiritual Warfare doctrine has developed. By that I mean, that there is the concept that we are to battle directly with the principalities, to the point where we name them, researching the history of cities and even nations, to learn the characteristics of these "strongmen" so that we could dislodge them, and "take the city for God."

Yonggi Cho, the pastor of the worlds largest Christian congregation, has taught the concept of an "open Heaven," in which the atmosphere has been cleansed of all demonic entities, and there is no hinderance to the Gospel. This has led to a number of symbolic actions by the church, in attempts to cleanse these heavens. These symbolic actions have ranged from fanning out across a major city in groups, to the highest geographical locations, including the top of buildings, and then at a set time, collectively proclaiming a rebuke to the perceived "strongman," to March for Jesus (whose founders admitted, was never about evangelism, but an attempt to "cleanse the heavenlies") to studying Greek and Roman mythology, on the basis that we need to know our enemies, and those gods are spirits. The ultimate end that this new spiritual warfare has brought us is "Identificational repentance," the symbolic acknowledgement and repentance of the sins of our ancestors to the descendants of those people whom our ancestors oppressed! C. Peter Wagner, in a *Charisma* article on the subject, stated that this is the church's power to "change the past!"

The new spiritual warfare is a whole lot more efficient than one on one evangelism, where you actually have to engage people with ideas, and you have to find out from them what they actually believe, this takes time and it is humbling, for you could be rejected! Why mess around on that level when we can go right to the top, the head honcho, the strongman! We are currently so anointed, we are actually mapping out whole nations, naming their prevailing spirits and focusing our energies against them!

The old paradigm for spiritual warfare was Paul in Athens, Corinth, Ephesus, or Peter in Jerusalem; they were "opening and alleging," debating and disputing, reasoning and persuading, to the Jews they would quote the scripture, to the Pagans they were willing to appeal to creation, conscience and even quote a few Pagan poets when they got it right on a given point. (Even a broken clock is right twice a day!) This is the meaning of 2 Corinthians 10, which speaks of "Vain imaginations, reasonings, thoughts, and knowledge that exalts itself against the knowledge of God." In short, their spiritual warfare was in the realm of the minds of men, challenging and engaging the philosophies, religions and emotional and intellectual barriers that prevented them from being saved. Paul didn't know that all he had to do was come against "Lust" in Corinth, Jezebel spirits in Jerusalem, "Witchcraft" in Ephesus, and "Intellectual spirits" in Athens. Paul was Roman citizen and yet he didn't even have the humility to apologize to the Greeks or Syrians on behalf of Rome, which had virtually plundered the whole world! He didn't counsel the Romans to do that either!

The new model is the Argentine revival, which the spiritual warfare people believe has come as a result of the new spiritual warfare practices. I quote Wagner again,

> "More than any place I know, the most prominent Christian leaders in Argentina, such as Omar Cabrerro and Carlos Annacondia, Hector Giminez and others, overtly challenge and curse Satan and his demonic forces both in private prayer and in public platforms. The nation as a whole is engaged in a world class power encounter."
> **(Engaging the Enemy** C.P. Wagner. Regal Books, p46)

This of course is a direct violation of the teaching of Jude 9 and 2 Peter 2:10 which warns us of willful, proud and boastful false teachers who are not afraid to despise dominions. And who are these dominions? Satan and the demonic hierarchy. "Whereas Michael the Archangel, when contending with the devil he disputed about the body of Moses, durst not bring against him a railing accusation, but said, the Lord rebuke thee, but these speak evil of what they know not" (Jude 9). Satan is God's problem, and God will deal with him in His own time and way.

So far, the weak view of salvation (without real conviction) has filled the churches with false converts, who need to be entertained and flattered. This has led to the prophetic movement. But one can only hear so many flattering prophecies, you have to feel like you are doing something significant. Evangelism is out of the question, it moves too slow, you have to be willing to think, and possibly be rejected, and the results are often dismal. Enter Spiritual Warfare! The dualistic nature of the new Spiritual Warfare, the attention focused on entities such as Jezebel, Saul spirits, the sins of ancestors and symbolic actions has opened the people to mystical new experiences, thus they will then be saying...

Didn't We Do Many Wonders?

We couldn't stay at any of these points for very long, for they are a river, moving along and they will take us somewhere. The mysticism of the new spiritual warfare movement, prepared us for the wave of mystical "revival" we are currently experiencing right now. Didn't we do wonders? Of course we have had to change our thinking in order to be able to receive this. Almost twenty years ago, John Wimber was calling for a paradigm shift in the church. A paradigm shift means that you change your paradigm, your world view, the whole way you perceive reality! John Goodwin, was a Vineyard Pastor almost from it's inception, and traveled extensively with Wimber for years. In his article entitled *"Testing the Fruit of the Vineyard"* he explains the paradigm shift that Wimber called for,

> "According to Wimber, in order for us to fully appreciate what God is doing in the world, we must experience what he calls a 'paradigm shift' from a Western way of thinking, to an Eastern way of looking at things...This paradigm shift is explained by Wimber in his seminar on 'Signs And Wonders and Church Growth' in what he calls a 'logic syllogism.' Presuming that people in the far east have an 'eastern' or experiential mind set, he describes an exchange of logic with an imaginary far easterner with the following result: You tell someone from the far or middle east that cotton only grows in warm, semi-arid climates. England is cold and wet. [Ask them] Does cotton grow in England? The answer you'll get is, 'I don't know, I haven't been to England.'"
> (*"Testing the Fruit of the Vineyard."* John Goodwin. Media Spotlight Report)

The shift is from a logical and rational approach to life to a purely experiential approach. This has done more to open people up to the current mysticism in Toronto and its offshoot, Pensacola, than anything else. In this new paradigm, the way God changes a life is redefined. Under the old paradigm of orthodox Christianity, "Truth shall set you free" and "The Son of God has come and given us an understanding" which also speaks of propositional truth. God has spoken unto us in His Son, He sent His Word, His *Logos*, and healed us. But the New Paradigm rejects all of that as necessary for a changed life, These days people are getting zapped! "I went down to Pensacola, and I didn't even believe in this stuff, but as soon as I came through the door, my legs started shaking, my arms started trembling,

I started twitching and ever since then, I have been consumed with a burning desire to be 'intimate with Jesus!'" Truth, in a logo-centric, propositional form, counts for nothing in the New Paradigm, it is "doctrine" and is for those churches that are dead, dry and "mainlining on prunes" as Rodney Howard Browne, "God's Bartender" likes to say. In the new paradigm it is no longer truth that changes lives, it is sheer experience. "Turn off your mind, don't pray, don't analyze, you wouldn't analyze a Kiss from your lover would you?" is how they put it up in Toronto.

Lord! Didn't we do many wonderful works? Toronto, and Pensacola were so wonderful they exceeded the revival in the Book of Acts! Peter and Paul never got whole congregations so drunk they couldn't stand up, but Arnott and Kilpatrick have! You talk about signs! When did John, James or Peter ever prophesy like a roaring lion, or fly around like an eagle?

Alas, you can't stay there for long, the party has to be over, the drunkenness has to wear off, the shepherds have to slumber, so that they can be like sleeping dogs, unable to bark a warning. What next? Then they will say...

My Lord Delays His Coming

And for this one, we have to turn to the book of Matthew 24:48-51. When the church begins to accrue the popularity and measure of worldly success and power, that it has, the Coming of Jesus Christ as an imminent reality loses its appeal. After all, what about the great last days revival? If Jesus came back tonight, what about all the prophecies that say we are going to come into a time where the average believer will be like Elijah, and our prophets and apostles will have names that nations will "Tremble at the sound of ?" "My Lord delays His coming."

"Christ isn't coming for us until He comes within us! We have to come into the glory, before the actual coming of Christ, so these "words" will come to pass! Don't talk to me about some "helicopter escape" out of here, with your old rapture theory! I don't want to escape, we are the cutting edged glorious advancing church!" And so goes the man exalting seduction, contrary to Jesus' solemn exhortation in Luke 21:36, "Watch ye therefore,

96

and pray always, that ye may be accounted worthy to escape all these things that shall come to pass and to stand before the Son of Man." With the loss of an imminent hope, there is a casting about for a new hope and meaning, which expresses itself in two distinct ways. One way your hope is in mysticism, an attempt at oneness with God, through sensual spirituality, "They will eat and drink with the drunken" which we have already noted.

The other way is the hope in a highly hierarchical church, "And shall began to smite his fellow servants." I look for the emergence of a new strain of the hyper shepherding movement, in a man-centered attempt to bring structure to the chaos that Toronto and Pensacola have wrought. "They will smite the men servants and the maidservants." Already their are signs of it, for the newly exalted prophets and apostles are assuming unique authority, there are now those who assume to be the "elder" or "apostle" of a given city. These positions have actually been conferred on them by the false traveling prophets! I was at a meeting of pastors in my city who had been invited to hear Rick Joyner. The pastor who had invited him actually told the assembled pastors to be sure not to miss the evening meeting, for they (he and Joyner) had been instructed to call the pastors forward, in order to "set them into the Body of Christ." The pastor of a large church in the Quad Cities has been radicalized by the new prophets, and is now given to an extremely aggressive tone, berating the flock, and telling them that if they don't like the "new thing" to "get out of my face, someone else wants your seat!" This behavior is actually applauded by that part of the congregation that has bought into this madness. Bill McCartney of Promise Keepers, when announcing to a stadium of men an upcoming Pastor's Conference, told them that if their pastor didn't want to support this, he needs to be able to tell them why not! There is a new strong spirit of arrogance. Partly this is because, I think, many pastors are feeling new importance by all of the self aggrandizing ministry they are bringing into their churches. But I also think that in the back of their minds, many of them are condemned because they have brought their churches into this mystical river, knowing it wasn't right, but afraid that they would lose out on all of the excitement, success, and popularity. Therefore in their spiritual hangovers, in between meetings and religious fads, they beat their fellow servants. God help them!

Is there any other way? Do we have to be carried down the river, to this end? I am sure that no one dreamed in the beginning that they would be at the point of screaming at their churches, to "Get out of my face! Others want your seat!" What pastor would drive away, in many cases some of the best people, people who have given their lives, time, money, and raised their children in the very church, that now berates them for not "jumping in the River?" What kind of revival is this? If there is another way to go, it would have to begin with humility. Let's face it— you have been bewitched. Go back to the Word of God, get away from the seducing notion that we are so special, that we are going to be great, and just be willing to become a redeemed human being again, washed in the blood of the Lamb, and under the Word of God. It may well be that there is still time to come back, to simple, beautiful, Orthodox Christianity. All we really have is Jesus and His promises, but that is all we have ever needed. I am no prophet, but I do offer you a proven Word from the Lord,

"In that day shalt thou not be ashamed for all thy doings, wherein thou hast transgressed against me: for then I will take out of the midst of thee them that rejoice in thy pride, and thou shalt no longer be haughty because of thy Holy Mountain. I will leave in the midst of thee an afflicted and poor people and they shall trust in the name of the Lord. The remnant of Israel shall not do iniquity, nor speak lies; neither shall a deceitful tongue be found in their mouth; for they shall feed and lie down, and none shall make them afraid. Sing, Oh daughter of Zion; shout, Oh Israel, be glad and rejoice with all of the heart, Oh daughter of Jerusalem, The Lord hath taken away thy judgements, he hath cast out thy enemy, The King of Israel, even the Lord is in the midst of thee" (Zephaniah 3:11 15).

Grace and Peace be with unto you.

In other words (combined with other sayings preceding this one), your child will reflect the sum of your thoughts at the time he is conceived.

| April 28, 1998: | The devil cannot manifest until you, the I am, connect your I am to that which is other than God. |

Jesus is the "I am," not man.

Encouraging self-love and speaking of how we allegedly create our own enemies as reflections of ourselves, Jordan leads into this one:

| May 23/24, 1998: | An enemy can only manifest as an expression of your own selfhatred. |

Didn't Jesus have enemies? Was he filled with selfhatred? He told us that the world would hate us if we followed after Him. Jordan's concept of hell is also telling:

July 9, 1998:	Your decisions will make your own heaven or hell.
July 10, 1998:	Heaven is a state of satisfaction, whereas hell is a perpetual state of confusion.
July 18/19, 1998:	Hell is not outside of God, but hell is in God.
August 8/9, 1998:	God and the devil are one.

This blasphemy reveals Jordan's god as the Force, possessing both a light and a dark side.

Of course, don't think that you can receive everything free from this "prophet." Every month contains repeated instructions on certain days that prompt the person to send money.

For example, each month has a "Special Offer":
Are you concerned about your family's destiny? Sow a $365.00 seed, and hear what God is saying about your family over the next year!
One day each month offers the following opportunity:
Send in your Miracle Seed of $98.00, your date of birth and

your most pressing question! I will prophesy your answer on cassette tape.

How much are you willing to bet that the cassette tapes contain generalizations to all possible questions depending upon the date of one's birth (and that multiple days of birth contain the same messages)? Maybe so, maybe not; I wasn't going to spend the money to find out how this astrological ploy manifests itself.

In addition to these monthly appeals for money, Jordan offers a series of audio tapes on meditation for $500, a number of workbooks for $50 per volume, and encouragement to register for the upcoming "Prophetic Congress" to be held August 24-27, 1999.

To charge money for a "prophetic word" from God is as evil as charging money for indulgences of God's grace, as has been the practice of Roman Catholicism. It was a major issue of the Reformation.

It comes as no surprise, therefore, that "Bishop" Jordan regales himself in a mitre hat, papal robes and a shepherds staff, as does the pope of Rome. The same spirit works in both.

Appendix 2

The Source of the River:
Are Toronto and Pensacola Equal?

The current revival movement which has swept the Charismatic and Pentecostal and even the evangelical world, is oft likened unto a river, even the River of God! The Psalmist tells us that truly, "there is a river, whose streams makes glad the city of our God," and all who truly love our Lord Jesus, do long for that river of living water. This is why we must seriously consider the claims of the proponents of the revival which broke out at the Brownsville Assembly of God, in Pensacola, Florida (BAOG). It would be presumptuous of us to simply dismiss the accounts of lives changed, dramatic encounters with God, and even decreases in the crime rates, of certain cities, as well as a host of other "signs and wonders." After all, many of us have been crying out for revival for many years, a revival is needed to shake the complacency that has plagued the church for too long. However, it would be equally presumptuous to "jump in with both feet," merely on the basis of the excitement that seems to be rejuvenating bored Christians and churches. We are commanded to judge all things, in the light of the scriptures. It would do us well to ponder the actual source of the "River," for in things spiritual, origin determines validity. Not only by their fruits, but by their roots shall we know them, "for a good tree cannot produce evil fruit, nor can an evil tree produce good fruit."

Where does this River come from? And where will it be taking those many thousands of believers and even churches, who have jumped into it? What streams flow into it, and into what larger current does it converge? There are divided views as to the meaning of this revival. Some see this as a sovereign move of God, and in some cases, the long awaited and prophesied, "Great last days revival." But there are others who imply, and in some cases come right out and say, that this is part of the "delusion" of Second

Thessalonians 2. Then there are those who take a third track, they don't care where the river comes from, to them all that matters are the apparent "results," that are occurring in many lives and churches. "It works, so don't knock it," in other words the end justifies the means.

This article seeks to answer these questions, and in particular the charge that the "River" is the direct outflow of what is known in apologetic circles as the Latter Rain/Manifested Sons of God heresy. My only qualifications are that I am a Believer, and a Pastor, who has written two books that seek to speak to similar and related phenomenon. My first book, *Making War in the Heavenlies, A Different Look at Spiritual Warfare*, written in 1994, was written to give my reasons for rejecting the spiritual warfare movement of the mid 1980's. Although I do believe that we are engaged in spiritual warfare, practices such as spiritual mapping, identifying the "strongman" over a given geographical location, challenging demon powers by name and rank, praise marches, driving stakes to claim cities for God, and a host of other practices that became intensely popular in the late 1980's and early 1990's, have more to do with magic and mysticism than they do with New Testament spirituality. When did Peter or Paul ever research the history of a city that they sought to evangelize, so that they could fight the "ruling spirits?" When did they ever challenge, curse or rebuke Zeus, Apollos, or any of the rest of the Pantheon? I assure you that they had ample opportunity!

My second book, *Weighed and Found Wanting*, dealt with the revival of outright mysticism, called the Toronto Blessing (TB) or the laughing revival. In my research, I found that the (TB) has descended from a long line of mysticism and erroneous teaching that goes back at least forty years. Starting with the Vineyard Movement itself, and moving back to the teaching of the late John Wimber, and further to the Kansas City Prophets, and their personal prophecies, and prophetic schools, also a man who dubs himself, "God's Bartender," Rodney Howard Browne, (heavily influenced by the Word of Faith error). The influences that have led to the TB, were varied, ranging from C.P. Wagner's church growth movement, and spiritual warfare teachings, all the way over to Paul Cain, the protege of William Branham, out of whose ministry came the Latter Rain/Manifested Sons of

God heresy, long since renounced by the Assemblies of God.

This is what brings us to our current subject, is Pensacola more of the same? Is this just another laughing revival, or Latter Rain? First I will give a brief account of the Pensacola Revival, especially a look at how it began, and the early influences. Then, a brief overview of MSOG teaching, which has infiltrated much of contemporary evangelical ministry, having captivated much of the Christian media.

The Pensacola revival, is the direct outcome of the Toronto Blessing, as the events that lead up to Fathers Day, 1995 show (the official beginning of the Pensacola revival). Previously, Steve Hill and the leadership of the Brownsville Assembly of God had gone up to Toronto to receive the "anointing" there. As the following article, (publication unknown) demonstrates, changes had already begun in the church, as a result of Brenda Kilpatrick's visit to Toronto.

"Strange, unusual and wonderful things started happening after Brenda Kilpatrick came back from the Vineyard church in Toronto, Canada... signs of early revival started manifesting in the spring services... What had been seen in Toronto started happening among the people of Brownsville... Brenda explained how she had a drastic change in her prayer life. 'I could never be the same again after I returned from Toronto.'"

She then proceeds to tell one of these 'wonderful things,' being frozen in one position for over two hours!

From several other inside accounts, it seems plain that this revival did not take anyone by surprise, there was a great deal of anticipation, that something along the lines of the Toronto blessing was going to happen at the Brownsville Assembly of God Church in Pensacola. The reason this needs to be emphasized is that one is often given the impression that "Suddenly, like a rushing mighty wind," the Spirit blew in on an unsuspecting Pentecostal church, actually hitting the Pastor in the back of the legs and knocking him over, and turning a one day preaching engagement into a three year series of continuous meetings, to everyone's complete surprise! On the contrary, it is obvious that something was expected of the

Steve Hill meetings. From the same article,

> "The time had come for God to allow his move at the
> Pensacola church, and Brenda explained how it came about.
> 'We had a friend named Steve Hill...he called us about his
> impartation that he had received from England. He was just on
> fire with a new anointing of what God had given him. We
> were so excited and said, 'maybe this will bring revival when
> Steve comes...'"

Like Brenda Kilpatrick, the pastor's wife, Steve Hill had also been to
Toronto to receive an anointing, having been prayed for by Carol Arnott.
But it was not until he received an anointing in an upscale Anglican church
in England, Holy Trinity Brompton, that the Pensacola revival was imparted
to Hill. Holy Trinity Brompton (HTB) church is the fountainhead for what
you are seeing at Brownsville, for it was there that Hill received his
anointing. Hill had first read about HTB in an article in *Time* magazine (of
all places) entitled "Laughing for the Lord."

> "Though pathetically tiny flocks of Londoners attend many
> Anglican services, Holy Trinity Brompton has a standing room
> only turnout of 1500...After the usual scripture readings,
> prayers and singing, the chairs are cleared away. Curate Nicky
> Gumbel prays that the Holy Spirit will come upon the
> congregation. Soon a young woman begins laughing. Others
> gradually join her with hearty belly laughs. A young worshiper
> falls to the floor, hands twitching...within half an hour there are
> bodies everywhere as supplicants sob, roar like lions, and
> strangest of all, laugh uncontrollably...this frenzied display has
> become known as the laughing revival, or Toronto
> blessing...After first appearing at Holy Trinity Brompton only
> last May, laughing revivals have been reported in Anglican
> parishes from Manchester to York to Brighton."
> *(Time magazine, Aug. 15, 1994, "Laughing for the Lord.")*

The very service that launched the Pensacola revival, was basically Hill's
recounting of how he received the impartation, at HTB. Hill was stopping

over in London, and was to stay with friends. Like many thousands of godly and dedicated ministers of the gospel, he was battle weary, tired and even spiritually hungry. Reading the Time article sparked something in him. He asked his British hosts, "Where is the Holy Ghost moving in England?" His hosts happened to be members of HTB, and they loaded him down with literature concerning the revival that HTB was experiencing as a result of Toronto. As Hill began to read, "testimony after testimony" of the lives changed and faith renewed, his hunger only increased. But he needed scripture, so he opened his Bible to the book of Acts and read "Have you received the Holy Ghost since you believed?" This seemed to be a confirmation, but he needed more, so he turned to another scripture, Aquila and Priscilla showing Apollos the more excellent way, which Hill interpreted them as saying, "There's More!" That was enough for him, so he made an appointment with the Pastor of HTB, Sandy Millar. Arriving at the church in the middle of a prayer meeting, Hill was amazed at the sight of it,

"I stepped over bodies to get to the Pastor. When Sandy touched me I fell to the ground. (I don't ever do that)...I was like a kid at TOYS'R'US...then I got up and ran to a couple and said 'Pray for me, man, this is good!' they touched me and WHAM! I went back down. Some of you God is going to hit in a powerful way. If you are hungry, get prayed for a dozen times."

(From the Fathers Day video, June, 1995).

In England and in much of the English speaking world, HTB is synonymous with Toronto Blessing. Even the secular press recognizes it, as you saw in Time magazine. The very name Toronto Blessing, was coined by a staffer at HTB. There has been much press coverage of the HTB/Toronto Blessing for example, in an article excerpt from a secular British publication entitled, *"Congregation Rolling in the Aisle"* by Nicholas Monson.

"It was my second visit to HTB and I was nervous... it was my friend Claire who reawakened my interest. She told me how the week before, the Holy Spirit had entered people in the church. She explained that this was because a church in Toronto had started to have visitations, and the enterprising clergy of HTB had flown over and literally seemed to have brought some of the Holy Ghost back with them."

And this from the *Daily Mail*, an article entitled, "*This Man Has Been Given the Toronto Blessing: What in God's Name is Going On?*" by Geoffrey Levy.

"[HTB] is a place of worship that has attracted large congregations... with verbal offerings by the Curate Nicky Gumbel such as 'Jesus blows your mind.' It must be said that soon after word of the Toronto Blessing reached them, that does appear to be what Jesus did."

The Christian press also, confirms this connection. *Alpha* magazine, a British evangelical publication, in an article on the TB entitled "*Rumours of Revival*" began with a description of a May, 1994 service at HTB. Charisma magazine, in a Feb, 1995 article entitled "*A Wave of the Spirit*" by Clive Price states of Vicar Sandy Millar that, "It wasn't until Millar went to Toronto that he experienced God afresh."

Steve Hill, himself, in an interview in *The Destiny Image Digest*, when asked to compare the two revivals, Toronto and Pensacola, replied,

"[Hill] Well I love John and Carol Arnott and I love Sandy Millar. I've been to both places and I believe they are both undergoing sovereign moves of God. I received a wonderful refreshing in Holy Trinity and I have been up to Toronto, where I had Carol Arnott pray for me. But we are dealing with different areas of the world...John and Carol Arnott came down here with members of their staff to visit us. When he said, 'Steve we want to see more of the evangelistic thrust,' I shared with him, 'God is using you brother, to touch the world right now. I don't think anybody needs to be duplicating anybody else, and I don't think that's the problem.' We've received a lot from the Toronto church on how to pray with people and care for folks. We model a lot of what is going on here from them."

As you can tell, there is a tendency to acknowledge Toronto yet at the same time to imply that there is a difference between the two revivals. But as I have demonstrated, Pensacola owes much to the Toronto Blessing. Not only did the leadership there make their own pilgrimages to the Airport Vineyard, the primary impartation that is the basis for the "river" came from HTB church, an Anglican church which was radicalized by the Toronto Blessing and became a major figure in its propagation.

Appendix 3
The crazy world of Gerald Coates

By Neil Richardson
including material taken from two articles in **Vanguard Magazine**
PO Box LB1475, Egham W1A 9LB UK

We live in a crazy world.
*(Gerald Coates, **The Vision**, p16; **Kingdom Now**, p76)*

In the 1970s the so called 'house church' movement began in England. Most of these churches operate under the banner of 'Restorationism', and show a commitment to restore the pattern of ministry of the NT churches, especially with regard to the ministries of Ephesians 4:11, including apostleship. Gerald Coates became a leader in the 'R2' branch of this movement: that is, the part that believes in fully engaging with popular culture as a means of evangelism, and also so that it may be enjoyed for its own sake. [see Andrew Walker's book, *Restoring the Kingdom*]

Gerald Coates, a former postman, now lives in a substantial country mansion at Cobham, Surrey. He and a number of other prominent leaders, such as John and Christine Noble and the eminent medical expert, Patrick Dixon, work together under the umbrella title of 'Pioneer' churches.

There is an emphasis in these churches on community action and social justice; prominent roles for women in leadership; demonstration of the supernatural gifts, especially tongues and the giving of prophecies, words of knowledge or 'pictures'; Vineyard-style rock-pop worship, with the worship leader being a sustained and central focal point; the 'slain in the spirit', 'carpet time', 'holy laughter' and other Toronto-style experiences.

The theology stresses the Holy Spirit; endtimes eschatology (namely, post-millennial Kingdom Now dogma, where the Church is expected to rise up and Christianise the world before the return of Christ); Revivalism; signs and wonders in gospel preaching (power evangelism); and—in the view of many—seriously underplays the authority of Scripture and the centrality of the message of Christ and Him Crucified.

Coates set up, with Roger Forster of Ichthus, Lynn Green of YWAM and the songwriter Graham Kendrick, *March for Jesus* which has now become a global phenomenon each summer. The thinking behind this is in line with another project of theirs, *Operation A-Z*. In both ventures, the view is that by moving geographically over the earth, somehow spiritual principalities and powers that are believed to be residing in or over these areas are vanquished. This is popularly known as 'claiming the ground', and is refuted superbly in a book by Chuck Lowe, published by OMF. The idea finds its most vocal manifestation in C. Peter Wagner of the Church Growth-dominated Fuller Theological Seminary in the US.

Coates has latterly furthered strengthened links with the US 'Prophetic Movement'. He has been staging for over a year now Big Top, US-style Revival meetings in Westminster, which he sees as a key location or 'spiritual stronghold' in England (as it is the seat of secular government). His fascination for this area led him to make a false prophecy concerning massive revival at Westminster Chapel, led by the Kentucky-born minister RT Kendall. This revival never took place, though Westminster Chapel under Kendall's leadership have gone further into the apostasy by linking up with Rodney Howard-Browne (originator of the Toronto Experience), Paul Cain (former Kansas City Prophet) and HTB, the church that first launched the Toronto and Pensacola experiences in England, and is responsible for the ecumenical and theologically defective *Alpha Course*, now almost universally acclaimed in the UK and worldwide as the *sine qua non* of evangelistic tools. At Coates' Revival meetings, several American personalities have peddled their wares, most notably Wayne Drain, Dale Gentry and Clark Pinnock, who has caused waves with his theology of God, in which he states that God neither has knowledge nor power over the future and—staggeringly—might even lose the cosmic battle against Satan were it not for our help. Coates has most recently shifted to the Royal Albert Hall, and is charging folks money to go and hear his stories of revival from around the world (by which he means the successful hyping of the flock into psychosomatic signs and wonders and group hysteria; this is perhaps most evident in South America under the leadership of such men as Claudio Freidzon).

Coates is also the author of several maverick and often self-regarding books, such as The Intelligent Fire (his autobiography- he is not yet 50), The Vision, Kingdom Now and Non-religious Christianity. From a brethren background, his criticisms of 'mainstream' or 'institutional' Christianity are not infrequent, and often not lacking in perception or grounds.

*With acknowledgements to **Charismatics and the Next Millennium**
by Nigel Scotland Hodder & Stoughton 1995*

Introduction

"Many Christians prefer to be spoilt by praise than saved by criticism" observes Gerald Coates in *The Vision*. This article fully intends to test Mr Coates' adherence to this principle! In an attempt to forestall the classic objection - 'yes, but have you read this by him... '- every attempt has been made to build up as broad and thorough a picture of Gerald and his teachings as possible.

The sources used are therefore:
'Gerald Quotes' (Gerald Coates, 1984, Kingsway; abbv: GQ)
An Intelligent Fire (Gerald Coates, 1991, Kingsway; abbv: IF)
Kingdom Now. (Gerald Coates, 1993, Kingsway; abbv: KN)
'Toronto' and Scripture (Gerald Coates, 1994, article in Renewal, reprinted in *The Impact of Toronto* edited by Wallace Boulton)
The Vision, an antidote to post-charismatic depression (Gerald Coates, 1995, Kingsway; abbv: Vis)
Non religious Christianity (Gerald Coates, 1995, Word Books, abbv: NC)
A Breath of Fresh Air (Mike Fearon, 1994, Eagle)

Charismatics and the Next Millennium (Nigel Scotland, 1995, Hodder & Stoughton; abbv: 'Sc')
Signs of Revival (Patrick Dixon, 1994, Kingsway)
The Pioneer website on the Internet (*http://ds.dial.pipex.com/pioneerpeople/*).
Evangelicals Now, July 1996 (Bulldog column) and February 1997 ('False prophecy today?')
Rumours of Revival video (presented by Coates, 1995, Word videos)
Sowing the Seeds of Revival videos (May/June 1997, with Coates and Dale Gentry).
A brief talk with Mr Coates at a Sowing the Seeds of Revival meeting (25 June 1997)
Discussion on Radio 4's Sunday the morning after the Wembley Stadium gig 'The Champion of the World' (28 June 1997)

Of this material, Scotland's *Charismatics and the Next Millennium* is highly recommended as an encyclopedia of the movement. *Rumours of Revival* is a inadvertently self-damning promotion of the Toronto Experience. *An Intelligent Fire* (Coates' autobiography) is probably the most astonishingly egotistical and self-regarding book I have ever read.

Gerald the Fabulist

Gerald has no fixed doctrine of revelation or of Scripture, and thence no clear understanding of the character of God. We must examine Gerald's 'pick and mix' or 'make it up as you go along' approach to theology. Gerald, like so many others, utterly reveres that "fat man just trying to get to heaven" (in his own words) the late **John Wimber**. This explains why Gerald goes firmly along with Wimber's "we are cataloguing all of our experiences so we can develop a theology". I suggest that the epidemic awe in which John Wimber is held by people like Gerald is not because of his sound, passionate Gospel preaching. It is not because of his soul-winning exposition of the Word of God. It is not because he has decided to glory in the cross of Christ (which initially was not mentioned in Power Evangelism!). It is because he gets 'results'. Jeremiah's lack of converts and Job's devastating losses would relegate both of them to the very bottom of the prophetic heap today. No, Wimber lives by faith, and look how big and successful Vineyard is. They have all the good music, and all the exotic experiences.

Gerald is also totally obsessed with numbers. What impresses him about Billy Graham is the 27,000 a night attendance (Earls Court, 1966). His unadvisedly-named 'Festival of Light' (is that a Hindu thing?) was fantastic because of the "30,000 who swelled Trafalgar Square [and] another group of several thousand" (IF, 83). Come Together ("a prophetic statement about the unity of the body of Christ" apparently) was held in Westminster Central Hall "crammed with over 2,500 people". We must commend Gerald for his incomparable ability to organise large groups of excitable people together, but numbers are very different from true spiritual fruit. And the hubris generated is unbearable:

> "If the house church movement was the most significant movement in the church in the seventies, the Nationwide Festival of Light and Come Together were the two major projects of the decade" (IF, 93).

Strange that the two major projects of the decade were both run by Gerald Coates, and that he doesn't flinch from telling us so in his autobiography. (It takes a lot of chutzpah to find your self a worthy subject of a book in any case, but as Gerald cites Anatole France, "A writer is rarely so well inspired as when he talks about himself". Gerald really should read the Bible: "Let another man praise thee, and not thine own mouth; a stranger, and not thine own lips" (Proverbs 27:2)

Gerald's ambition for big crowds following him about is seemingly insatiable. [Gerald doesn't seem to mind citing this comparison of him with a certain German chancellor... "Mr Gerald Coates, who kept the continuity between the different parts of the rally, often encouraged the audience to give its festival salute, in the form of a raised arm and hand, rather reminiscent of the salute performed at a different sort of rally just over thirty years age."] He's now succeeded in filling Wembley Stadium, the largest venue in the UK ('The Champion of the World' 28 June 1997). Where next?! But I have to confess, isn't there some confusion as to who the champion is? The Lord Jesus for His sacrificial death and triumphant resurrection, or Gerald for filling a stadium of happy clappers?

The problem with a results-and-numbers-based theology is twofold. First, "if I still pleased men, I would not be a servant of Christ" (Galatians 1:10) and "woe to you when all men speak well of you, for so did their fathers to the false prophets" (Luke 6:26). Second, when the numbers aren't there, what's going to become of us? Our security is not in the Lord, but in 'how many we can influence'. Gerald will increasingly find that in order to fill stadia, he will have to "heap up for them teachers. .. and they will turn their ears away from the truth, and be turned aside to fables" (2 Timothy 4:3-4). Gerald is proud to be a storyteller, a fabulist, if it gets bums on chairs: "I'm a prophet, not a Bible teacher."

But just what kind of prophet is Gerald?

Prophecy 1: "Dr Kendall—in eighteen months from this month (April 1995) your church. Westminster Chapel, will be unrecognisable, completely and totally unrecognisable... the Holy Spirit will increase in power [*How can the Holy Spirit of God increase in power? Only other spirits can have their influence enlarged or diminished by God's sovereign permission. NR.*] In 18 months (October 1996) the Spirit of God—not just upon Westminster Chapel, but upon Westminster itself, upon the high of the land, upon many who live in that area, is going to come on that place and many of your prayers—taxi drivers would get out of their taxis because the Spirit of God is so strong in that place—you're going to see them fulfilled. And it will come from the most unlikely sources, it will not come through the people you would like it to be through, it'll come through the most unlikely sources. And if you keep your heart and your eyes open the Spirit of God is going to surprise us all." (Given at Spring Harvest, April 20 1995; circulated by Kendall at Westminster Chapel in December 1995).

Outcome I:

"What has come of the prophecy [which] states... in short, that the area and the church will have been transformed by revival? [What has happened] appears to be the complete reverse of what was promised. Far from experiencing joyous revival it is reported that over 100 people have left Westminster Chapel since Dr Kendall's well-publicised attempt to bring the Toronto Blessing on the church. There are the dwindling numbers in the church, the continuing lack of impact on the local community and the complete absence of a godly direction taken by many among the Parliamentary 'high of the land' . Sadly, in anyone's book, this is tantamount to the failure of the prediction. If the prophecy did not come from God, then are we not constrained by God's Word to declare that they are the vain imaginings of a false prophet?"

(Alan Howe, 'False prophecy today?' **Evangelicals Now,** *February 1997 - essential reading).*

The writer of this article can verify this- I was one of the 100+ who left West Chap (ask to leave RT Kendall's office as the preacher raged at my daring to question the Biblical soundness of Toronto). West Chap is a shell of its former glory, and the preaching of the Word is mingled with abortive attempts to stir up the 'double anointing' that RT desperately craves as, sadly, his ministry flags.

Here's what the Bible says:

I. If you prophesy something that doesn't happen, under Mosaic law, you are put to death.

"But the prophet, which shall presume to speak a word in my name, which I have not commanded him to speak, or that shall speak in the name of other gods, even that prophet shall die. And if thou say in thine heart, How shall we know the word which the LORD hath not spoken? When a prophet speaketh in the name of the LORD. if the thing follow not, nor come to pass, that is the thing which the LORD hath not spoken, but the prophet hath spoken it presumptuously: thou shalt not be afraid of him"

(Deuteronomy 18:20-22).

How does Gerald get round this? He has made a false prophecy, declared something in God's name which didn't happen and brought "the reproach of the heathen our enemies" (Nehemiah 5:9). Under Moses, he would already be dead. Is he sorry? Not a bit of it! He told me that West Chap was unrecognisable! Well in once sense he is right, if you want to destroy the significance of words forever. It's a bit like some builders coming round to do up your house and promising to leave it 'unrecognisable'. You didn't place quite the same emphasis on the word when they scarper leaving it a complete bombsite which is spiritually what Westminster Chapel is. Why can't Gerald face up to the fact that he's made a serious error (a resigning offence) and repent with humility? Because his ego and the credibility of his own word stand higher in his estimation that the warnings of Scripture and the plain facts of the matter.

2. Don't listen to prophets God hasn't sent, who fabricate fine prospects about the future with their imaginations.
"Do not listen to the words of the prophets who prophesy to you. They make you worthless; they speak a vision of their own heart, not from the mouth of the Lord. They continually say to those who despise me, 'The Lord has said, "You shall have peace"'; and to everyone who walks according to the imagination of his own heart, 'No evil shall come upon you' ... I have not sent these prophets, yet they ran. I have not spoken to them, yet they prophesied—how long will this be in the heart of the prophets who prophesy lies? Indeed they are prophets of the deceit of their own heart, who try to make my people forget my name by their dreams... Behold I am against prophets who use their tongues and say, 'He says.' ..."
(Jeremiah 23- more topical reading you will not find!!).

Prophecy 2.
"In 1991 Mr Coates visited New Zealand where he informed local church leaders that God had spoken strongly to him about an earthquake that would devastate Lake Taupo. The leaders were told this would take place in April of that year. Local Elim leaders believed this prophecy and instigated a national media campaign to warn their nation. 44 Elim churches began taking survival courses. April came and went

and nothing happened [*Nigel Scotland confirms this: "Gerald ... prophesied that a volcano would erupt in NZ by a particular date. It Didn't Happen (Sc, 151)*]. The secular press had a field day laughing at the church and particularly evangelicalism"

Ibid **Evangelicals Now**

Outcome 2:

The earthquake didn't happen. IT DID NOT HAPPEN. What did Gerald tell me? "Because by the faith and the prayers of the leaders the earthquake was diverted"- without blinking twice! Why did they take survival courses then? Did Gerald mention anything about this in his prophecy? No.

Stunningly, Gerald decides to edit out of the Bible the bit about things not happening as being a mark of a false prophet: "No, the judgement of death on the prophet is not only given for words that do not come to pass, for there are several interpretations of what could have happened or might yet happen. A false prophet is one who leads God's people into open rebellion and idolatry. Rebellion against God and his word. ..I would suggest that almost all prophecy is conditional if not all" (*Kingdom Now*, 129-130). This appalling doctrine of convenience is akin to the prosperity gospel 'if you're not healed, it's because you lack faith, not because I lack integrity or power'. As Alan Howe correctly points out:

> "Taken to its logical conclusion, this argument makes all prophecies completely untestable". *(ibid)*

And that's just the way Gerald wants it, especially seeing as he sets so much store by the bogus, discredited Kansas City Prophets—notably Paul Cain who "gave a prophecy which later caused great confusion and a fair amount of disillusionment among many thousands of Christians in Britain. He declared that revival would break out in London in October 1990" (Sc,151). Of course, Cain and Wimber (who supported the prophecy until it proved itself utterly untrue) wheedled their way out of it by saying that Wimber "had misunderstood Paul Gain who prophesied 'tokens of revival' as implying something of much greater proportions" (ibid.). The sheer nerve of Coates, Wimber and Cain takes one's breath away. They make up in audacity what they lack in veracity! They may be liars. but they're brilliant at following through the bluff.

Prophecy 3,

"There is no doubt that we are seeing the early stages of 'a world revival.'" (Patrick Dixon, Coates' whitecoat henchman—great on medical ethics, terrible about the operation of the Holy Spirit [*He believes that Altered States of Consciousness...are the basis of dynamic, personal, relevant, living faith" (Signs of Revived.* 260)].

Outcome 3:

Each successful wave of the false fringe of the charismatic movement has claimed that revival is 'just around the corner'.

With rising disenchantment. Gerald has decided to manufacture his own revival. Rodney Howard-Browne style, in 'the heart of the UK', Westminster. and in Wembley Stadium. Complete with Dale Gentry, the sub-Rodney double, asking for people to be in a "posture of receptivity" particularly to his demands for money which take up a substantial part of the meeting—where the preaching of the Gospel used to go in real revivals. Rodney's, 'line-'em-up-and-knock-em-down' technique is enjoyed by many, as is widespread untranslated tongues ("But if there be no interpreter. let him keep silence in the church: and let him speak to himself. and to God" I Corinthians 14:28). Gerald tries his hand at a bit of Benny Hinn 'blowing the anointing' but looks a bit disgruntled as he doesn't seem to have the same devastating effect as Hinn or Hinn's role model, Kathryn Kuhlman. In the absence of any message whatsoever (except that the 'christian' pop group *Delirious?* are in the Top Ten). The only gospel that can be preached is the gospel of 'revival'—that is weird ecstatic experiences and general mayhem. Revival has replaced the Lord Jesus as the key word. The whole experience is a bizarre mixture of the terrifying and the unutterably boring, which seems to me the quintessence of hell. I tried to help a girl who was attempting to drink from a bottle but could not because 'God' had made her jerk and shake so alarmingly she couldn't get it to her lips. Many professing non-Christians went to the front to be zapped with the 'Holy Spirit' (despite the fact they haven't repented and don't know Christ at all), and got up again absolutely none the wiser about the person of the Lord Jesus Christ—the only means of their salvation. Apart from anything else, a perfect opportunity for the true Gospel is disgustingly wasted every night (this is a six-week revival, you see). The violence of Dale Gentry as he dragged people to the floor had to be seen to be believed, as well as his quite obvious use of kundalini yoga chakra points on people's bodies (especially the 'crown chakra' on the top of the head. which is said to govern spiritual receptivity and the chakras at the belly and the base of the spine). Kundalini may or may not be a genuine psychic/demonic power, but it certainly helps to push someone over if you've got a hand on their head. and the other on their back!

"And many will follow their destructive ways, because of whom the way of truth will be blasphemed. By covetousness they will exploit you with deceptive words" (2 Peter 2:2-3).

Gerald, like Nicky Gumbel, does not acknowledge that there is false teaching in the church, only 'Pharisaism' from those who are earnest to discern "the spirit of truth and the spirit of error" (I John 4:6). The Pharisees were never interested in the Truth. They didn't even recognise Him when He was talking to them! In fact their preoccupation with having a large group of followers was their downfall! "If we let him thus alone, all men will believe on him: and the Romans shall come and take away both our place and nation" (John 11:48). The big-shot cult personalities have hijacked the term 'Pharisee' and have misapplied it to all those who dare to question their ministries. But the truth of the matter is that their fixation with empire-building and earthly recognition is far more Pharisaical than those they threaten.

We end with a few quotes from Gerald that both he and we would do well to put into practice:

• "We create a high trust factor... [by] honouring our words and promises" (*The Vision*, 128)
• "The Apostle Paul made it clear that even the prophetic church will only 'know' in part" (ibid.154)
• "Some of the things I said, both privately and publicly, were what I wanted to believe had happened. Accountability was needed" (!!! *An Intelligent Fire*, 81)
• He also says in a couple of places how he rejects untranslated tongues (never mind the fact that the 'Sowing the Seeds of Revival' videos start with several minutes of it).
• He resents speakers with their 'thus sayeth the Lord' approach. Dale Gentry, however, is entirely backed by Coates as he proclaims that "the Holy Spirit spoke to me last Thursday and said, 'There's a revival in Westminster.'"

That is to say, we've given up waiting and hyping so let's just pretend it's here and if we shout loudly enough. maybe the people will believe us.

As Gerald quotes at the beginning of his chapter, 'The Visionary': "Where there is no vision the people are unrestrained... " (Proverbs 29:13, NASB).

Let us earnestly petition the Lord that He may restore restraint, truth, vision and real blessing to a church direly in need of Biblical reform, that we might "repent and do the first works", especially in proclaiming the simple power of the Gospel of the Lord Jesus Christ!

As I write this, I feel increasingly burdened that we respond to the issues raised and the people concerned with discernment and compassion in equal measure. It is frighteningly easy to fall into either the camp of 'it's all over, the global deception is here' heresy hunters, or the 'welcome the new dawn of world revival' charismaniacs. The Truth Himself promised His Spirit, and that He would "guide us into all truth" (John 16: 13). We must work so, so hard at learning how to speak that truth in love, so that all sincere believers "may grow up in all things into him who is the head- Christ" (Ephesians 4:15). We all have a lot of growing up to do: some of us need to consider "whether we want to win [people over] or simply point out their error"

(Coates, *The Vision*); others of us may want to think about whether we care about truth at all. We all need the Lord's tremendous grace that we might daily demonstrate that "love which covers over a multitude of sins" (Proverbs 10: 12, I Peter 4:8).

For those (like me!) prone to seeing leaven in every lump, check out the admonition to the Ephesian church in Revelation 2. For others who tend to see more with rose-tinted specs than with the eyes of discernment, don't miss the message to the church in Pergamum in the same chapter (especially verse 15).

One final comment: if you come away from reading this concerned about Gerald Coates, put it into action in praying for him and those whom he influences. If you come away feeling offended or outraged, please pray for me!

"Let the words of my mouth and the meditation of my heart be acceptable in your sight, O LORD, my strength and redeemer" (Psalm 19: 14).

Appendix 4

The Two Mysteries

"We are in that kind of age today. It is becoming more and more of a psychic age. It is an age of the soul just spilling over, asserting itself, taking control of everything Christian as well as outside of it--a soulish age...Be careful that you are not hankering for this realm again. Are you after the evidence? My, how I have seen dear Christian people just prostrating themselves with groaning and crying, almost screaming for evidence--these 'sign' things...Christians and dear men of God, who have been greatly used, are creating an emotional, psychic situation that is involving simple Christians in things which are, sooner or later, going to be a great disillusionment and an offense. It will bring 'offendedness' with the Lord, and that is just what the Devil is after."

*(T. Austin Sparks. **Called Unto the Fellowship of His Son**. Page 46.)*

These are interesting times. If someone would have told me 20 years ago, that the end of the millennium would be a time of extreme and diverse religiosity, I wouldn't have believed it. At that time, the overarching concern for Christians was the specter of an ever increasing secularism, which looked with disdain on religious devotion as "outdated superstition."

"Secular humanism" was the "Goliath" taunting us Christians. But now look around you. Are we not living in the most religious time in recent history? Spirituality has made a comeback and it seems to be back with a vengeance! In this "Post Modern" era, all religious opinions are treated as equally valid in the name of tolerance. Eastern religion, Zen Buddhism and even Kabbalah and Ramadan, are respectfully being treated in today's media and by sports figures and celebrities. Even within the Church of Jesus Christ, there seems to be a revitalization of the "old time religion." The overnight expansive growth of phenomena such as Promise Keepers, March for Jesus, the Toronto Blessing, Willow Creek Church and other various expressions would seem to indicate (as many Christian leaders proclaim) that we are in the "great last days revival," and that these are the greatest moves of God since the days of the apostles!

Far from being atheistic and materialistic, America seems to be more spiritual and God-conscious then ever. This recent flood of spirituality requires all of us to make choices, to discern. At some levels, the choices for believers are obvious: blatant Christianity or blatant mysticism, Eastern religion or paganism. At other levels, they can be quite difficult, for example, is Roman Catholicism Christian? Should we have the Pensacola "anointing" in our church? Should we be part of the "city wide church?" Am I to *pursue* racial reconciliation as a Christian?

These are just some of the serious issues coming across through Christian media and requiring thousands of ministers and tens of thousands, even hundreds of thousands of Christians worldwide to be for or against.

Hopefully, this article can be a help to you who love the Lord Jesus and seek to be faithful, both to His call for His own to be united in love, as well as His command and warning to be discerning, even critical, in these last days. I would say at the outset (since I do believe these are the last days) that the great issue which confronts the flock of God is neither unity, nor power signs and wonders. The question is not, "Will the churches ever come together like the Lord prayed in John 17?" Nor is it, "Will we ever have the power to do signs, wonders, and miracles like the book of Acts?" The issue is **Truth**. Will we receive the love of the truth or will we believe the lie?

Even him, whose coming is after the working of Satan with all power and signs and lying wonders. And with all deceivableness of unrighteousness in them that perish; because they received not the love of the truth that they might be saved. And for this cause God shall send them strong delusion, that they should believe a lie; That they all might be damned who believed not the truth, but had pleasure in unrighteousness.
2 Thess 2:9-12.

Though indeed there are so many different spiritualities flourishing in the world today, there are in essence only two religions underlying them. All

124

religious expression or experience can biblically be put into only two categories, two spiritual principles or mysteries as the bible calls them. They are either the Mystery of Godliness or the Mystery of Iniquity. As far back as the Garden of Eden (and even before that) these two spiritualities have coexisted.

The first of these two mysteries to appear in scripture is called the Mystery of Iniquity. It found its first expression in the very Mount of God, in the Garden of God where Lucifer the angel of God proclaimed his now infamous "I Will's"

How art thou fallen from heaven, O Lucifer, son of the morning! How art thou cut down to the ground, which didst weaken the nations! For thou has said in thine heart, I will exalt my throne above the stars of God: I will sit also upon the mount of the congregation, in the sides of the north; I will ascend above the heights of the clouds; I will be like the Most High. Isaiah 14:12-14

Now this is the essence of iniquity, lawlessness, that the created being can assert himself up out of his God assigned role, by an act of his will, to become equal with God! This spiritual principle, this essence of all false religion, starts with the creature, who would "ascend up to heaven." You can follow this all through the Bible and human history to this present day. Adam and Eve, willing to believe that they could be "like God" even if it meant trampling love, loyalty, commitment and gratitude in the dirt, as they grasped their own "personal fulfillment." Nimrod, whose very name means "Let us rebel" (*The Genesis Record*, page 251, Henry Morris, Baker Book House), organized a worldwide revolt against the binding restrictions of the God of the Bible and could only be stopped by the catastrophe of the confusion of tongues at Babel--they wanted to "ascend up to the heavens," "to make a name for ourselves." This is the ancient lie, the recurring temptation of fallen man which countless pyramids, ziggurats, meditation techniques, Masonic degrees, gurus, Christian Scientists, Mormons, New Agers, Yogis and countless other world religions testify to, that somehow or other "man can ascend up to God's level and be like God." This principle of creaturely ascent is at the heart of all false religion including the occult, for all time and in every culture. It is the Mystery of Iniquity.

The Mystery of Godliness however, is the opposite of the Mystery of

Iniquity. If Iniquity says, "Man can ascend and be like the Most High," Godliness says, "God must descend and become a man" in order to save us who are desperately lost, completely bankrupt, and unable to save ourselves." This is the spirituality that originates from Heaven and which requires an incarnation, "God was manifest in the Flesh." There can be no compromise, nor mixing of these two religions. The scriptures warn us that the two would coexist, mature and come to their fullest expression in the last days before the bodily return of Jesus Christ. The spirituality of iniquity, whose motto could be "Let us (creatures) ascend." or the spirituality which produces godliness which would have the opposite motto, "He (God) must descend to us."

And no man hath ascended up to heaven, but he that came down from heaven, even the Son of man which is in heaven. John 3:13

In the light of these two simplified definitions of the two respective mysteries, godliness and iniquity, we can take a critical look at recent spiritual developments within the church. In 1992-1994, as the pastor of a small Pentecostal church in Cedar Rapids, Iowa, I was made aware of a new surge of interest in spiritual warfare. I could always accept as biblical the concept that as believers we are engaged in a tremendous spiritual warfare. This has been the position of orthodox Christianity all the way back to the apostles. I have never had a problem with the ministry of deliverance, the "casting out of devils" for I've seen that this also was proscribed by the Lord and His apostles. However, in the new superspiritual warfare, we have something unique to the teaching of the New Testament. Christians are being told to "rise up into the heavenlies and do battle with the strongmen" over cities and even nations! The title of my first book reflects this new "belief." *Making War in the Heavenlies,* comes directly from a popular song being sung in worship services which touts that "We are making war in the heavenlies, we are tearing down principalities." Notice the emphasis is what We are doing as the church, through Jesus (of course).

Contrast this with the orthodox Christian view of spiritual warfare, which is a battle of cosmic proportions indeed but which is in the realm of ideas, thoughts, belief systems, etc. Christianity has taught that Satan blinds men, through "vain imaginations, high things, that exalt themselves above the knowledge of God," and that Christian warfare is to dismantle these mental "strongholds" through the truth of the Word of God. This takes time, patience, love, dedication, prayer, commitment, and humility. We see Paul, in the Book of Acts, engaging in spiritual warfare.

And Paul, as his manner was, went in unto them, and three sabbath days reasoned with them out of the scriptures. Opening and alleging, that Christ must needs have suffered, and risen again from the dead; and that this Jesus, whom I preach unto you, is Christ. Acts 17:2-3
Therefore disputed he in the synagogue with the Jews, and with the devout persons, and in the market daily with them that met with him. Acts 17:17
And he reasoned in the synagogue every sabbath, and persuaded the Jews and the Greeks. Acts 18:4

This is spiritual warfare according to the Bible, teaching, discussing, arguing, and reasoning scripture, dismantling the intellectual and philosophical barriers to faith in Jesus Christ. If Paul had the modern teaching of spiritual warfare, he would have been researching the history of the respective cities, trying to identify the spiritual entity which controlled it. He no doubt would have discerned a spirit of adultery in Corinth, witchcraft in Ephesus and a spirit of religion in the city of Jerusalem. Acts 17 tells us that when Paul arrived at Athens, "His spirit was stirred in him when he saw the city wholly given to idolatry..." What was his response? Did he scream at Zeus or bind Apollos? Did he gather a citywide meeting of Greeks and apologize to them on behalf of the Romans? Did he march around Athens and plant stakes at the four corners of the town to claim it for God? These are just some of the recent "revelations" that have come forth of late and which are being practiced in the name of spiritual warfare! But Paul knew from the gospel that there is only one lowly method of doing spiritual warfare, "He disputed daily in the synagogue with the Jews and with the devout persons, and in the market daily with them that met with him." Acts 17:16-17.

The two approaches to spiritual warfare come from two different sources, or spiritual principles. I discern the Mystery of Iniquity in this new spiritual warfare. Remember it's motto, "Let us ascend" up to God's level. "**We're** making war in the heavenlies, **We're** bringing down principalities!" Kenneth Hagin, the "Word of Faith" leader, tells a story about a visitation he had with "Jesus." "Jesus" came to him supposedly, to give him some direction and instruction, but a demon imp materialized between Hagin and "Jesus" and began to raise such a racket Hagin couldn't hear what Jesus was saying to Him. Hagin relates that after waiting for "Jesus" to rebuke the demon and observing no apparent response from "Jesus," Hagin himself rebuked the imp and sent him away. Then this "Jesus" told Hagin, in effect, "If you hadn't done that, I couldn't have!" This new "Jesus" doesn't presently have all power and authority for He has, according to Hagin and others, delegated it to us, the believers. Therefore it is up to us, not Jesus, to complete the plans of God.

Bill Hamon articulates this doctrine in his book, *The Eternal Church*,

"Jesus is waiting on the church. All that the fall of man and sin has taken away from humanity, Jesus through His church shall restore"
"When the church has put under it's feet all enemies of Christ...**then Christ can be released from Heaven** to return as the manifested head of His physically resurrected and translated church."
(Prophets and Personal Prophecy, Bill Hamon)

In the old and true spirituality, we, the church, are waiting for Jesus to come back to "redeem the purchased possession," and to complete our salvation. But, in the Mystery of Iniquity, as always, all is reversed, **Jesus has to wait for us**, the church, to rise up in our power and glory, and to take dominion over all and when **we** get to that place of unity and power, ruling and reigning, then He can come back so that we can hand the kingdoms of this world over to Him. John Wimber, at a Docklands, England 1990 conference said,

"There is something higher than being a [Denomination] and that is to be the end time army and involved in this greater prize of bringing everything on earth and above the earth and below the earth to the feet of Jesus."

This dangerous doctrine has far reaching implications in that it seriously alters the world view of all who submit to it. Bill Hamon, John Wimber and a host of other popular leaders widely influencing the church confuse the person of Jesus Christ and the church. Hamon says, "When the church puts under its feet all enemies of Christ." While Wimber looks to the "greater prize of bringing **everything** on earth and above the earth and below the earth to the feet of Jesus." Wait a minute! Where does the New Testament give us that kind of mandate? I Cor 15, Psalm 110, and Psalm 2 tell us that Jesus is the one who will do these things, or that God will do them for Jesus, nothing is said of "The Great Last Days Church" rising up and performing these wonders!

The effect of this rapidly spreading delusion, is to exalt man and confer upon us the prerogatives that belong to Christ alone. I've tried to document this trend in my book *Weighed and Found Wanting* which I believe is the direct outcome of the once rejected 'New Order of the Latter Rain Movement'. It, in turn, was influenced by its offspring, 'The Manifested Sons of God Movement', both of which were denounced by the Assemblies of God in 1950. The Latter Rain Movement taught that this last days church would be the greatest expression of the Body of Christ ever! Through "The Great Last Days Outpouring of the Holy Ghost" the church would supposedly come into the time of the greatest power, unity and effectiveness ever! The Manifested Sons of God Movement sprang out of that and taught that Romans 8:19 would be fulfilled before the coming of Jesus, that an elite group of Christians would be so perfected by revelation that they would come into a complete "manifestation of their sonship" and overcome all, even death, before the Lord's return. Once again I believe you can discern by now which Mystery energizes this, "Let us arise" up to God's level and take dominion, we can be the greatest demonstration of the church ever! Though this idea was denounced it never went away. From the late 1940's till now it has consistently developed and resurfaced in many different ways. From Latter Rain to Manifested Sons of God to Kingdom Now to the Word Faith Movement to some aspects of the Church Growth Movement, definitely Spiritual Warfare, the Prophetic Movement, (we currently have a Restored Apostles Movement) and I believe definitely Toronto and Pensacola are mystical manifestations of the same basic premise, that **without** the bodily return of Christ, the church will somehow develop, and perfect herself and come into glory and honor and power, of course all in the name of Jesus, but without His coming, and that we will be dominant and influential as a church in this world, before the coming of Christ. Lest you think I exaggerate, here are a sampling of current teachers' comments: Bill Hamon prophesies of the day that:

> "The President of the United States and heads of nations will begin to seek out the Christian prophets and prophetic ministers...to know what to do...The Joseph and Daniel Prophetic Company will arise with supernatural answers for the...Egyptian Pharaohs and Babylonian emperors of this world."

In his "Harvest" 224 page prophecy, Joyner tells us that as the last days church, we carry "the credentials."

> "The feet of the Body of Christ will carry the credentials for all those who have gone before them. They will be joined to each other like no other body of people have ever been joined...In the near future the church will not be looking back at the first century church with envy because of the great exploits of those days, but all will be saying that he certainly did save his best wine for last. The most glorious days in all of history have now come upon us. You who have dreamed of one day being able to talk to Peter, John and Paul are going to be surprised to find that they have been wanting to talk to you."
>
> (Rick Joyner, **"The Harvest."** Page 26)

Is the church getting better and better over time? Are we evolving? Are we about to "breakthrough" to the greatest church ever in history?

According to the Mystery of Iniquity we are, but the Mystery of Godliness doesn't teach so. How can the church get better, when she's always been "complete" in Christ? Is God comparing the 20th century church to the first century church? (I hope not.) The church has no generations, it has always been composed of individuals who are in various stages of personal growth in Christ! Are we the first generation to "invent spiritual mapping", "identificational repentance" or command the Holy Spirit to come to us? The apostles knew nothing about these things, have we evolved past them? C. Peter Wagner tells us in his spiritual warfare book, *Engaging the Enemy*, page 46, that the reason for the revival in Argentina is linked to spiritual warfare.

> "But more than in any other place I know, the most prominent Christian leaders in Argentina such as Omar Cabrera, Carlos Annacondia, Hector Giminey and others, overtly challenge and curse Satan and his demonic forces both in private prayer and on public platforms. The nation as a whole apparently is engaged in a world class power encounter."

Which of the two spiritual principles is being operated from here? The Mystery of Godliness or Iniquity?

Yet Michael the archangel, when contending with the devil he disputed about the body of Moses, durst not bring against him a railing accusation, but said, The Lord rebuke thee. Jude 9
Whereas angels, which are greater in power and might, bring not railing accusation against them before the Lord. II Peter 2:11

The effect of this "new revelation" is to puff us up with pride and blind us to reality. The Mystery of Iniquity is like that, "Let us ascend!" sounds better to sinful man than "God must descend" to save us. This is the time Jesus warned "take heed that no one deceive you" and yet with all the binding, loosing, commanding, cleansing the heavenlies, singing militant songs like "He's under our feet!" and so forth, deception seems to be the remotest possibility to "cutting edge" Christians.

The very essence of biblical spirituality is this, God had to come down to us, in the flesh, God became a man, to save us from sin. The very antithesis of it, is this Mystery of Iniquity, this principle of **man ascending** up unto God's class. The polarization of Christians along these lines is upon us, and the choice is becoming increasingly stark! In closing, Jesus poses a question which I believe is directed to the last generation of believers, that on the one hand, to some incurs serious heart searching, but on the other hand, to the "new breed," the question is almost irrelevant in the light of the great and mighty "revival" of signs, wonders and power sweeping the earth. The question is: "Will the Son of Man find faith when He comes to the earth?"